MW01240654

OOMPH! Press © 2022

This English language translation is published under First Serial Rights. Original author, publisher & translator retain full copyright.

The original French language text was provided courtesy of Paul Dakeyo and Alexandre Khaïr-Eddine.

Edited by Daniel Beauregard & Alex Gregor
Cover design by Daniel Beauregard & Alex Gregor
Layout by Alex Gregor

For a complete listing of titles please visit www.oomphpress.com

RESURRECTION
of WILDFLOWERS

RESURRECTION OF WILDFLOWERS

NOTE FROM THE TRANSLATOR

[« Au moment vrai tout meurt, tout redevient puissant »]

"At the very moment everything dies, everything becomes powerful once again"

- Mohammed Khaïr-Eddine

*

I finished the initial draft of Mohammed Khaïr-Eddine's *Resurrection of Wildflowers* sometime in the late fall of 2020, in north Philadelphia, where I'd been living waywardly over the past year. Unbeknownst to me at the time, the end of that particular year would mark a period of life-altering endings and beginnings for me, including, among other things, relationship upheaval, abandoned career prospects, the deaths of family and of friends, and of friends of friends, and a process of relocation that would ultimately find me on the opposite side of the continental United States, from which I had originally started.

Although I can draw only faint comparisons between my own life and that of Khaïr-Eddine (forced from his home country at a tender age and into a precarious life abroad, exasperated by poverty and xenophobia), the fact that his publication of *Resurrection of Wildflowers*, and my subsequent translation some 40 years after, were both rife with personal upheavals and resultant homecomings is too coincidental to resist commentary. I am fascinated by the ways that the lives of the translated and the translator coincide and even intertwine across extreme gulfs of space and time.

*

Originally brought to print in 1981 by Éditions Stouky in Rabat, Morocco, *Resurrection of Wildflowers* marked more than just the publication of a new volume of poetry for Mohammed Khaïr-Eddine. True to its name, it marked a resurgence, a revitalization, a veritable resurrection of one of Morocco's most daring poets: one that was as personal as it was artistic. For 14 long years, from 1965 to 1979, Khaïr-Eddine had been living in and around France in self-imposed exile from Morocco, finding solace in the intellectual circles of Europe, particularly Paris, where he had established a name for himself as the author of numerous full-length novels, poetry collections, and difficult-to-categorize hybrid works.

However, in 1979, the distance from his homeland must have proven too much for Khaïr-Eddine, and he made the decision to leave France.

Knowing full well that he would be risking persecution for the subversive activities to which he had contributed prior to his exile (among other things, co-founding, alongside Abdellatif Laâbi and Mostafa Nissabouri, the highly influential and eventually banned radical left socio-political literary magazine *Souffles-Anfas*), Khaïr-Eddine returned to his native country of Morocco.

Resurrection of Wildflowers is the book he chose—the first book he chose—to publish upon his return. A vertiginous maelstrom of Moroccan, Maghrebi, Amazigh, and African-inflected imagery, *Resurrection of Wildflowers* marked, for Khaïr-Eddine, a total re-immersion in the native soil from which he had physically distanced himself for so long and the sum of his experiences that he had carried with him while abroad.

Resurrection of Wildflowers is that special kind of book that oozes from an author's very pores.

*

At the climax of my personal strife, I remember taking an impromptu getaway to the ominously named—but no less beautiful—Worlds End State Park in northern PA. What I remember most vividly about the trip: the sprawling wildflowers that lined the highways for miles and miles leading into the park, despite the seemingly inhospitable conditions. Fascinated by their ornateness, I wondered why and how these wildflowers chose to grow in such abundance almost exclusively in roadside ditches, where they found themselves bombarded by people and traffic and all the pollutants that follow. After recounting my experience with some ecologist friends of mine upon my return, I found out that wildflowers are peculiar little things. Unlike some more finicky varieties, they thrive where they can, when they can, often choosing nutrient-poor or otherwise disadvantageous soils because they, unlike some other varieties, have inside them the impetus and the resiliency to flourish in extreme conditions. And though they tend to live a relatively short life, it is a glorious one, full of color, and renowned by and accessible to many. This thought was a great comfort to me at the time, as I expect it must have been for Khaïr-Eddine as he chose the title for his collection.

When I think of myself and Mohammed Khaïr-Eddine both coming back to where we began our lives—he to Morocco to publish *Resurrection of Wildflowers*, and I to the Pacific Northwest to finish my translation of it—I feel tangled up in his life and history, thankfully and rewardingly propelled by it. Walter

Benjamin famously speculated that "a translation proceeds from the original. Not indeed so much from its life as from its 'afterlife.'"* But where does the translator proceed? Surely, they are changed utterly—resurrected—in much the same way that a text in translation is resurrected. It seems to me that translators understand a great deal of death, just as they do of revival. With every decision they make or do not make, they catch a glimpse of death, momentary as it may be, deciding what is and what is not to make its way into this proverbial afterlife. I don't know that a translator can define themselves as having "proceeded" from a given translation. That is, I don't believe that a translator can define themselves against the person they were or the life they led before translating a given work and the person they were or the life they led after translating a given work. All that said, I don't believe that a translator does "proceed" from a translation, or if they do, they do so like the undead. The translator is an interloper of lives and afterlives.

If poets are "the unacknowledged legislators of the world,"** as proposed by the English poet Percy Bysshe Shelley, then translators could be said to be the unacknowledged legislators of death. I have always respected Benjamin for abstaining from ascribing any light or darkness, good or bad, or positive or negative attributes, to this afterlife. Every afterlife, like every poem, and perhaps especially every translated poem, is inscribed with both gains and losses, joys and sadnesses, and lights and darknesses. There is the faintest glimmer and glimpse of truth and then the continual, desperate resurrection of that faintest glimmer and glimpse. Mohammed Khaïr-Eddine knew this to be true. The trope spins like a fractal throughout his work, no less so throughout *Resurrection of Wildflowers*, which finds the author

[avec ces rêves sanglés,
m'oxygénant atrocement, répudiant de ma rétine
l'ombre et l'éclair d'ombres abouties au soleil.]

alongside these drawn-back dreams,
forcing the air atrociously into [his] lungs, spitting from [his] eye
obscurity and obscurity's illumination, both ending in sunlight.

---

* Walter Benjamin. "The Task of the Translator." *Selected Writings, Volume 1: 1913 – 1926*. Edited by Marcus Bullock and Michael W. Jennings. Harvard University Press, 1996, 254.

** Percy Bysshe Shelley. "A Defence of Poetry or Remarks Suggested by an Essay Entitled 'The Four Ages of Poetry.' *Shelley's Poetry and Prose*. 2nd edition. Edited by Donald H. Reiman and Sharon B. Powers. WW Norton & Company, 2002, 535.

For Khaïr-Eddine and his poetry, obscurity and illumination are the bedfellows of perception. It is within this seeming paradox of embracing light and darkness that one ultimately sheds light on truth. The perception of truth must travel into and out of being, unraveling life and death, utterly enmeshing the seer in it, until it can't help but seep, however ephemerally, from their very eyes.

*

Abstracter musings aside, I want to take a moment to dwell on some of the nuts and bolts of this translation. Beyond the complex imagistic wilds of *Resurrection of Wildflowers* lay an equally complex sonic field, and this field deserves commentary. As a translator, I've made the choice to "resurrect," first and foremost, and to the best of my ability, the sonic quality of his text, as that sonic quality seems to me to be the river upon which the onrush of Surrealist imagery travels.

Keen observers moving between the English and French texts will note that I've implemented more punctuation in the English translations than was originally present in the French. Khaïr-Eddine's punctuation in the French text is often erratic and irregular. This is no defect, however. His ear is shrewd, and the placement of said punctuation, along with his choice of vocabulary, especially his choice of vocabulary, is both a deliberate and precise act toward generating his desired music. The reverberations between his words steward that music, particularly the embellishment of internalized rhyme. Take, for example, the following passage:

[Toujours l'enfance amère retournée dépecée
sur les soieries du labour et du chant,
hésitante mais sautillant entre mes doigts
sur les cupules où le rêve me foudroie.

De quelle menace narguer le dard acerbe
et le tordre le tordre contre les cloisons
de la nuit épouvantable qui désherbe
ce pays au fond de tes yeux comme un poison?]

Forever that bitter childhood returning, churning
over the laborious and song-filled silk factories,
hesitating, before shooting through my fingers
into my cupula, where the dream like lightning strikes.

What threat is mocking that acrimonious sting,
this writhing, writhing against the cloisters
of night's colossal shroud, pulling this country's
weeds up like poison through your bottomless eyes?

("Plowing in Kan," *Resurrection of Wildflowers*)

Although no punctuation is present in the first line of the French text, there is a necessary rhythmic pause forced between the heavily stressed endings of "retournée" and "dépecée." Similar pauses are forced by the rhymes of "chant" and "hesitante" in the proceeding lines and even further where "tordre" appears before the grammatically discontinuous repetition of "le tordre," where the rhythmic caesura is forced through the sheer rotundity of the word (generated by the *r* sounds in close proximity). Khaïr-Eddine does not eschew punctuation for the sake of eschewing punctuation but rather because his lexicon performs the heavy lifting of his prosody in a far more elegant way than could the superficiality of grammatical conjunction.

As sounds coalesce, every poem pulsates like one long guitar string, every word in every one of his poems like a delicate coil in that longer string. The sounds travel along with ease, from beginning to end. Because there is no direct equivalent to be had when interpreting the French into English, it is difficult, if not impossible, to approach the music via vocabulary alone. To do so would be to expect the same sound out of a violin as one would an oboe upon the performance of musical notation. More instruments from the English language were needed for this orchestra.

*

For both the reader's sake and mine, I will restrain from accounting further for my each and every decision in translating, offering only a glimmer and glimpse toward what I've decided is a suitable "afterlife" for the time being: that which remains after *Resurrection of Wildflowers* pours through my pores. To say any more than that would be disingenuous. Just as some of my instinctual decisions as a translator remain a mystery to me, some of Khaïr-Eddine's decisions remain a mystery to us all, and it's that very mystery that lends the volume its ultimate strength.

*

While some things remain unclear about the text, it's perfectly clear to me and I hope to others that *Resurrection of Wildflowers* is a text that was near and dear to Khaïr-Eddine's heart. Indeed, it was one that the author himself did not think twice about resurrecting. In fact, in 1994, he would release an updated edition of the book, this time by way of Éditions Nouvelles du Sud, run by French-Cameroonian poet and fellow comrade Paul Dakeyo. Although Khaïr-Eddine would not alter the original ordering of the 1981 volume, nor edit any of its individual poems, he would add a number of new poems to the end of the original edition, breathing a breath of fresh air into the collection.

The text that appears here in translation is based on the full 1994 version, presented with as much care and fidelity to the author's original vision as could be surmised from a side-by-side comparison of both books' respective idiosyncrasies. It is with great pleasure, pride, and humility that I and OOMPH! Press present this book to the English-speaking world.

*

Here's to hoping that Mohammed Khaïr-Eddine has many more lives (and afterlives) to come.

- Jake Syersak

Mohammed Khaïr-Eddine: Hooligan of Letters
Translated from the French by Jake Syersak

I met Mohammed Khaïr-Eddine two or three times by way of Jacqueline Arnaud, who introduced us. A little tipsy, he paid me little attention, despite Jacqueline's insistence that we exchange a few words. I'd just released *Le View de la Montagne* from Éditions Sindbad, and still, I was very intimidated by the Maghrebi poet, whose work often astounded me in the same way Kateb Yacine's did. I said next to nothing each time, and never sought him out thereafter, knowing that I might always find him at the Sélect in Montparnasse, where he had built up an infamous reputation, one which he cultivated like a great lord.

Most everything that I'd known about him came from Arnaud or Edmond Amran El Maleh, who would sometimes allude to "his smile, forewarning an explosive phrase,"* and later from Pierre Joris and Malek Alloula. But all that said, it is perhaps not so terrible an idea to take a step back from the physical presence and biography of the author, in order to take the time needed to investigate the body of work they've left behind, and to seek out no explanations other than what the text itself happens to suggest.

If Kateb Yacine's writing is "the malediction" of colonial domination, according to the formula suggested by Nabile Farès, that of Khaïr-Eddine's would, in my opinion, be the insurrection and the excess of language in opposition to what has been ordained and then clearly displayed in a world in decomposition. Tahar Ben Jelloun labeled it "a guerilla warfare of words,"** emphasizing its laborious subversion and the techniques of ambush intrinsic to the poet's speech:

> I charge ahead with the verve of a cemetery,
> gold-digger of darkness, master of moons dealt a deadly
> blow.

> ("A Love Letter to the Angels Who Aren't Listening,"
> *Resurrection of Wildflowers*)

Indeed, for Khaïr-Eddine, "digger of invisible gold,"*** the "poet is an eternal

---

* Edmond el Maleh, "Mohammed Khaïr-Eddine: Poète Libertaire," *Horizons Maghrébins: Le Droit à la Mémoire*, 1996, n°30, 129.

** "La Guérilla de Khaïr-Eddine," *Le Monde*, June 18, 1976.

*** Toni Maraini, "Mohammed Khaïr-Eddine: Orpailleur des Ténèbres," *Horizons Maghrébins: Le Droit à la Mémoire*, 1996, n°30, 129 – 131.

dissenter," one who retains "the genetic memory of the cosmos."* This memory, eaten away by fire, is inscribed on a body—"an ordinary body" over which "the cataclysms of the city cast themselves" ("The Weariness of Atta," *Resurrection of Wildflowers*)—hurtling towards "the unknown by way of a derangement of one's senses," as advocated by Rimbaud.** This, however, by way of patient, rigorous, and innovative formal work, starting as far back as his first major published poem, "Black Nausea":

Syllable by syllable I build my name

It is from here that Khaïr-Eddine's dissidence begins to grow into a louder expression of what it is, without succumbing to the banalities of so-called "serious" writing.

Present ever since the launch of the *Poésie Toute* manifesto with Mostafa Nissaboury in 1964 and the first texts to appear in the literary journal *Souffles*, established by Abdellatif Laâbi in 1966, this interrogation of the existing order was only to grow in frequency throughout the course of his publications. The escapades and overindulgences of man, exotic and remarkable as they may be, hold little in common with the dissent advocated by the poet in his writing, a dissent that is not always politically contextualized, but whose subversive scope remains exceptional and current to this day. It draws its strength from an unconventional prosody and metric in a language where every so often the images and rhythms are enough to upend and divert the set course of one's reading.

A fine connoisseur of Rimbaud, Khaïr-Eddine appropriates his "Alchemy of the Word" ("At first it was an experiment. I wrote the silences, I wrote the night, I recorded the inexpressible. I fixed frenzies in their flight.")*** to translate his world into its own language. The poet is aware of his expanding the visionary poetics originally put into motion by Rimbaud and the Surrealists, as he once confided to the Mauritian poet Édouard Maunick: "To begin with, had we not the genius of the language and, in spite of all its sentimentality, its combined power of evocation, we could not have yielded anything outside this linguistic force and this unprecedented rhythm, both of which assure us that not one of our texts carries any residues of déjà vu."****

What is essential here is not the seeking out of originality at any cost

---

* Interview conducted by Abdallah Bensmaïn, in *L'Opinion* (sup. culturel), September 24, 1982.

** "Letter of the Seer" to Georges Izambard, May 13, 1871.

*** Arthur Rimbaud, "Alchimie du verbe," *Une saison en enfer*.

**** Interview conducted by Edouard Maunick, *Demain l'Afrique*, Paris, May 7, 1979.

but the necessity of translating a new language into a reality grasped in fragments and fulgurations, to render the movements of life visible, to make felt all those pulsations and trances capable of overwhelming one's visionary senses.

In his own words: "To restore life, which is action, you must know how to unearth the right words, to create the adequate formulas and forms, as well as new forces. You must reinvent a universe, starting from diffuse, almost non-existent materials."* Indeed, this is the task of Mohammed Khaïr-Eddine's entire oeuvre which, in order to extract said words, digs deep into language, into exquisite and explosive corpses, allowing him to restore his inner world, a world that began in the small Amazigh village of Tafraout, in southern Morocco, that "dreadful desert," that obsessive and mystical space inscribed in his blood:

my black blood once the blazing milk in the breasts of the desert

("Black Nausea," *Arachnoid Sun*)

It is a blood that he would try to render visible throughout his poetic production, defining himself as *Sudique* (*sud* [south] + *ique* [ish/esque/escent/etc.]):

Sudique in my delinquent image
in my blood that beats without a heart

("Sudique," *Proximal Morocco—*)

A neologism to mark the unique feature of the man of the South, exiled to the North, where he will come to know disenchantment:

The South explodes into a thousand rapiers
disheveling your every nerve…,
and the swing plow reigns over the doldrums of stone people
wandering about, suspended from the stars, disintegrating.

.   .   .

Later, I discovered the world as it is.
("Swing Plow," *Resurrection of Wildflowers*)

It is the emptying-out of this magical universe of childhood that the poet will fill with rage. Violence sweeps over nostalgia, and it is with the harshness of a

* Interview conducted by A. Aibour, *Itinéraires et contacts de cultures*, Paris, 1991.

Lautréamont or a Césaire that the words come surging forth, "doubling down with ferocity," with a tempestuous flood, to say what exile seeks to stifle. The poem is a backlash against the erasure of those tracks, the stance permitted to the ante-Islamic, whose rhythms, lushness, and lofty lyricism Khaïr-Eddine retained, questioning the desolation of place without lingering too long, this requisite of a world living in the exuberance of the moment, the premises of a fugitive future.

As Khaïr-Eddine himself explains, "When I write, my texts exude the scents of the entire country, its tastes and even its peculiar animal world...Its argan trees, its venomous snakes, its deep, dry wells, its wild rockfaces, all that lived on in my work, even in exile":*

> It was her heart that beat here once, amid this scree of stone,
> amid the nopals and euphorbia, their yellowish milk...,
> amid the thistles and blazing wildfires of summer
> consuming nothing but rock, quartz, and soil, dismayed
> by the lengths that hate will go to.
>
> ("Underneath the Forgotten Pomegranate Trees,"
> *Resurrection of Wildflowers*)

But exile is not so much what torments this nomadic poet, this "strangeness of a thing that drifts on by," forever on the move and forever integrating himself into the locales to which he sojourns, in search of that "word that stops dead in no one's eye."** It is this search for the reckless word, common or erudite, that Khaïr-Eddine pursues unceasingly. The audacious word that neither sacrifices polysemy nor ambiguity and which is characteristic of the poet's wanderings.

Resurrection of Wildflowers, published in 1981 in the city of Rabat by Éditions Stouky, comprised 59 poems. Reprinted in 1994 by Éditions Nouvelles du Sud in Ivry-sur-Seine, 17 poems were added after "Fibula," the final poem of the earlier edition. A "description" heads up the volume: "Here is a poetic exploration marked by a period extending from 1976 to 1990." The title of the collection takes its name after the 53rd poem of the book, a veritable "Invitation to the Voyage" and "Drunken Boat" to launch one toward and into the unknown:

> My blood is this strangeness of a thing that drifts on by...
> a well-rigged vessel, its sail torn to shreds

* Interview conducted by Kadhim Jihad, *Al Yaom Essabiï*, April 10, 1989.

** Mohammed Khaïr-Eddine, "Mémorandum," *Soleil arachnide*, Éditions du Seuil,1969.

by the the night's obsolete winds.

("Resurrection of Wildflowers,"
Resurrection of Wildflowers)

Meanwhile, the poem that opens the collection, "From Casablanca to Bogotá," is a lamentation-imprecation and revolt against the torment perpetuated against "women / and children, the elderly, the city, even the sea!..."; the poet rails against the misery of those left behind, against the fate of the natural world and those who would "overload" it with catastrophe, without, however, taking an explicit Third-Worldist or ecological position, leaving the reader to make do with "the unobservable word," along with the name of the three cities to which he alludes: Casablanca, Bogotá, and Beirut...

AS IF THE SUN ITSELF WERE NOURISHING DEATH!

("From Casablanca to Bogotá," *Resurrection of Wildflowers*)

This revolt figures into the poetic whole that makes up the collection, into its haunting leitmotif, accentuated by the unusual resonances of the chosen vocabulary and the subtle deployment of consonantal interior rhymes.

But why select, for the title of the collection, a poem that does not seem to occupy a particularly remarkable space in the construction of the book? A blurring of the lines, particular to the writing of the larger collection, whose beings, places, and things interpenetrate one another "on the wall of memory," like an exorcism purging the return of the evil spells of exile. With no remorse or nostalgia, the poet prepares himself, without ever revealing himself entirely, to embark upon a new stage in his perilous life:

> For I've found second wind in this new blood, rigged
> beyond recognition, sails in the breeze, and I'm arming it to the teeth.

("Resurrection of Wildflowers,"
Resurrection of Wildflowers)

The "description" referred to above proposes one reading: "These poems read like the history of a world in perpetual transfiguration." A proposal oriented, perhaps, towards an essentialist vision, which is not usually the case when it comes to

Khaïr-Eddine's poetics, a poetics firmly anchored to the continuous movement of the world rather than to its transfiguration. The poems of this collection are deeply rooted in the reality of his native Moroccan South and the places he visited, the Koranic prosody and the mystique of the Maghrebi *tasawwuf* infusing his verse, bestowing it with that "convulsive beauty" sought by the Surrealists. From this perpetual movement, which is a permanent transformation, the poet gives shape to erratic images and an aggressive rhythm that subverts any cursory reading. While it comes to fruition, he watches, entangling time and space, allowing pieces of its mystery and chance to remain in place, having understood well the lessons of Mallarmé.

The final poem in *Resurrection of Wildflowers*, "Recourses," dedicated to Lahbib M'Seffer,* ends with an injunction to shed oneself of everything that would obstruct being, so that one might coalesce with nature, the habit being the simple garment of the Sufi, whose errant quest leads to the annihilation of the self (*fanâ'*):

"Drape yourself in this habit!, O habitual evil."

The sea itself awaits
the sound of a nova's drawn bow.

A disconcerting injunction if one interprets it in a mystical sense, whereas for Khaïr-Eddine it's up to the poet, "moored to [his] blood...[and] skin,"** to raise his head and offload whatever is superfluous, so that he might persevere in his quest for the mot juste, by way of yielding inner-being to the natural world surrounding him.

- Habib Tengour
Iowa City, Saturday October 23, 2021

---

* Khaïr-Eddine met the painter in 1988. He published an article on him, "Lahbib M'Seffer, peintre bucolique," in *Esprit*, in June 1992, and a book in 1994:,*M'Seffer vu par Khaïr-Eddine*, Arrabeta Editions, Casablanca.

** "The Strangeness of the Passerby," *Resurrection of Wildflowers*

RÉSURRECTION des FLEURS SAUVAGES

Mohammed Khaïr-Eddine

RESURRECTION
of WILDFLOWERS

Translated by Jake Syersak

À FRANCOIS PATRIMONIO

FOR FRANCOIS PATRIMONIO

DE CASA À BOGOTA

Ces peuples se tuent à graisser les entrailles
du diable !
Se tuent-ils pour rien ? Non !
Ces peuples, oh ! mon enfant ! de Bogota à Casa
de Casa à Bogota
s'en vont ensemble quérir du ciel un sale reproche !

Ils errent, dissemblables, ils errent sous des haillons
silencieux que le soleil colore ;
ces peuples atroces rêvent que la nuit bleue
s'éparpille en étoiles simples sur vos flibustes ;

et tous, les yeux éteints, voient passer la rivière,
les grands sacs, les vieux mythes, les pires délires,
les séismes et les fruits qu'ils n'ont jamais cueillis ;
et tous avec la nuit chantent et se démembrent
pour ne faire qu'un avec le ciel uni.

Ce ciel qui dévore ta mémoire, qui te réprime,
ce ciel sans qui tes mains s'embrancheraient au sol,
ce vieux ciel que l'on te fourre dans la tête,
horrible ciel jamais atteint, triste sourire
par où ton sang neuf est goulûment sucé,
enfant, oh ! mon enfant ! que diable ! tourne la page
et vois le vrai ciel en ton âme assassine !

De Casa à Bogota, de Bogota à Beyrouth,
le sang siffle la précaire
flûte de ces bergers sicaires qui briment l'enfant,
la femme, le vieillard, la ville et même la mer !...
et dont la parole grince sur mon trident...

L'actinie hérisse ses lignes écrites depuis toujours
et le nuage dérobe à l'éclair foudroyant

FROM CASABLANCA TO BOGOTÁ

These people, just dying to grease the entrails
of Satan!
Dying for nothing? Hardly!
These people, oh!, my child!, from Bogotá to Casablanca,
Casablanca to Bogotá,
they go hand-in-hand in quest of a filthy tête-a-tête with the heavens!

Wandering, disparate, wandering out beneath the silent
hand-me-downs dyed in sunlight;
these atrocious people dream that the night's indigo
gets strewn into unquestionable stars, capstones of your fleecing;

and everyone, light extinguished from their eyes, watches the river go by:
the enormous trash bags, the age-old myths, the deluges of delusions,
the seismicity, and the fruits gone unpicked, left to rot on the vine;
consigned to night, everyone sings, and rips each other limb-from-limb,
conforming to the form of the heavenly expanse.

These heavens devouring your memory, crushing you from above,
without which your hands, down below, would branch out,
those old heavens, leaving their scorch-marks inside your skull,
those awful, unattainable heavens: that wallowing grin
through which your blood gets sucked, voraciously,
child, oh!, my child!, enough!, leave this hell behind you
and behold the true heavens: your soulful assassination!

From Casablanca to Bogotá, Bogotá to Beirut,
blood whistling through the precarious
flute of Sicarian shepherds, tormenting women
and children, the elderly, the city, even the sea!...,
whose speech squeals against my trident...

The actinia stirs, standing its timeless lines on end,
and clouds steal away with the lightning

cette terre inepte où tu gis sous une pierre
avec dans la bouche un mot amer
et autour du corps des couteaux qui se détendent !

Amour vaste et qui déteint sur toi,
petit imbécile incendié par un sourire !
Fou des mares gîtant, recréant, t'extirpant
des noces du tonnerre juste qui t'envenime.

Mais ceux qui se souviennent regardent sauter le monstre,
l'inobservable mot qui, prononcé, sous-tend
la terre et ses musiques, les oiseaux et leurs rémiges
éventées par l'aboi inépuisable du Rire !...

et du feu, tant va l'eau sur moi, calamiteux,
radié des ténèbres, éclaboussé du spectre
infinitésimal qui te frappe de cécité ;
alyte, avec tes œufs, c'est la terre murmurée
et le grand cénotaphe oublié et la Mère
qu'épouvante le sable et que troquent les scinques !
Je les vois vivre enfin ! s'éliminer, j'entends !

chacun depuis hier et avant le crépuscule
disant : "moi ! moi !" râpeurs ! soûlauds ! pillards !
et tournant autour des filles comme autour d'une lampe
le vague insecte, l'insecte suicidaire !

COMME SI LE SOLEIL DEVAIT NOURRIR LA MORT!

Parce qu'ils tremblent et tombent, parce qu'ils noient
leur chien,
parce qu'ils crachent sur le ciel qui est un puits !
sur le ciel assis en nous et dans leur sang !
ils réenfantent et tanguent, ils te surchargent, Terre,
du mal sorti de tes viscères !

over this inept land where you bury your head in sand,
and into your tongue, a stinging word,
and around your body, sequentially relaxing razors!…

One vast love, whose colors are rubbing off on you,
you inconsiderable fool, set alight by a smile!
Crazy about the listing pools, reproducing, rooting you out
from the wedding of righteous thunderstorms, envenoming your veins.

But those who can still recall the moment the monstrosity sprung up,
that unobservable word which, when pronounced, underpins
the world and its music, the birds and their feathers
all brought to light by the inextinguishable howl of Laughter!…,

and fire, flowing like water over my body: a catastrophic,
shadowy radiation, awash in the infinitesimal
specter that strikes you blind;
midwife toad, eggs in tow, earthly murmuration,
great forgotten cenotaph, grand Mother
scaring up the sands, soon to be swapped out by skinks!
Finally, I see them in the flesh!, liquidating themselves, and I listen!

Every one of them, day after day, facing down the twilight,
saying: "Me!, me!," Rapists! Drunkards! Looters!
And then, spinning around the little girls, as if around a lamp,
that unknown insect, that suicidal insect!

AS IF THE SUN ITSELF WERE NOURISHING DEATH!

Because they tremble and go tumbling, because they are unwinding enough rope
to hang themselves with;
because they spit into that very well they've chosen to call the heavens!,
because the heavens are welling up inside them, inside their blood!,
they are welling up to poise themselves for a second birth, to overload you, Earth,
with a sort of evil, an evil sort spewed from your viscera!

LE RÉMOULEUR

Il fit un rêve où il se trouva maître
du fil fin du couteau —
il glissait dessus le premier vers
ce désert où stationnent tes reîtres

son chemin m'éclaboussait
et sa tête geignait — ruineuse
de soi comme des lames marines —
son corps tombait en multiples copeaux

j'étais couché dans le cambouis
mangeur des anciens panicauts
son œil crevait les chromosomes
qui gigotaient dans ton désert

un peu de sang mon dieu un peu d'urine
nous ne pouvons boire autre chose
si le lait des mères le rend lugubre
donne-lui le ciel qui te sclérose

il n'y avait même plus de larmes
dans la cave de ses désirs
il n'y avait que ce couteau
cette fausse route pour l'occire

chantre charmeur de vieux babouins
ton anneau délicat se rompt
sur les carcans et sur les clous
que ma tête abrupte fêle

je sais l'histoire de l'orphelin
qui but la rivière boueuse —
il germera dans les prisons

THE SHARPENER OF KNIVES

He had a dream in which he was master
of the knife's razor-thin edge—
one glided over the other on its way to
this desert where your cavalry stood in wait

the path he forged washed over me
while his head gently whimpered—self-ruining
like the sharpened swells of seascapes—
his body falling away in slice after slice after slice

I'd laid myself out among the filthy oils
the swallower of ancient eryngo
his eye would crush any chromosome
that wormed its way through your desert

just one drop of blood my god just one drop of urine
we cannot slake our thirst on anything else
if mother's milk is what gets him so gloomy
lend him a little of your heavenly paralysis

there were no more teardrops
in the deep cave of his desire
no more than this knife
this flawed way of slaying

O cantor O charmer of old baboons
your delicate ring breaks
on the shackles and nails
my precipitous head cracks

I know the story of the orphan
who drank of the muddy river—
he flowered inside the prisons

et les pierres de tes palais

il marchera sur tes vieilles rides
lorsqu'à travers lui tu verras
l'homme qui glisse sur l'éclair
le rémouleur et le couteau

and the stones of your palaces

he shall make his way across your shriveled skin
and through his eyes you shall come to see
the man who runs the sharpener of knives
and knives alike across the lightning

SOUS LES GRENADIERS OUBLIÉS

Ici la terre et la mer aigrissent de conques
ton cou brisé par les lances du soleil ;

les murs de la ville très bas réveillent l'arbre
ou l'arganier sur les pleurs des mères fleuries
de troglodytes murés et d'onces suant sur moi
plus pavé qu'un ciel orageux plus hystérique
que ton ombre, soleil qui défies ma pensée.

La femme portant la montagne sur son dos
la femme naissant du creux moite de l'omoplate
des moutons sacrifiés sur l'ardent miroir fauve
se lardant de joie acérée se lardant
de galets morts sur ma langue de galets noirs
ourdis contre l'œil sur une plage...
nous étions étendus voyageant dans ton sourire !

Dorade ! Licornes et narvals, hommes-lyre, oiseaux,
loups !
La scolopendre, fétu dictant aux glèbes
une mort aussi sereine que mon regard !...

                                        Larme
de mère issue de plantes fourragères, ô
incompatiblement mûr pour toi, très mûr,

                                   je vais
par ce chemin abrupt atteindre tes yeux blets !
Ici où la terre et la mer se fatiguent.
Entre les roseaux, Elle... Moi gisant... Un figuier
nous tend ses fruits mûrs.
                          Ciel
et nuages !
          Et très haut

UNDERNEATH THE FORGOTTEN POMEGRANATE TREES

Here, the entirety of the earth and sea is busy curdling your neck
into seashells, broken up by the hurled-down spears of the sun;

The insurmountably sunken walls of the city give rise to the foliage
through which the argan tree, fed by weeping mothers, blooms
with cloistered troglodytes and leopards, whose drool above me
looms, smoother-paved than heavenly maelstroms, more hysterical
than your shadow, O sunlight gone against the grain of my thought.

Woman carrying the mountain across her backside,
woman emerging from the clammy hollows of scapular
sheepfolds, sacrificed to the mirror's fauvist intensity,
transpierced with a double-edged joy, transpierced
by the dead cobbles befalling my cobbled-black tongue,
plotted against this beachgoer's eye…
our bodies outstretched, traversing the length of your smile!

Sea bream! Unicorns and narwhals, lyre players, birds,
wolves!
The scolopendra, the feeblest wisp chanting a death
serene as my own gaze across the glebes!…

        A mother's

teardrop descends the foraged crops, O
too impossibly ripe for one so ripe as you,

         I descend

the steepness of this slope, awaiting your overripened eyes!
Here, where earth and sea wear one another down.
Among the reeds, She… I, lying motionless… A fig tree
extending us its ripened fruit.
      The heavens

and the clouds!
    And higher up,

une lune peut-être qui pose ses nasses
avec sa langue concassant nos étoiles.
Mortes ? Non ! Fatiguée de l'amour âcre
non consommé...

Les roseaux frissonnaient en noces de tambourins
la dans des hommes au fond du puits teintait
de sang
la fille sortie de mon corps comme un tonnerre.

Son petit ventre rose dans l'eau claire du torrent,
ses petits seins pareils aux grenades éclatantes...
tout son corps baignait dans un ruisseau de sang.
Loin de moi cet harmattan ! Vent d'orage ! Inepte tribu
de démons turbulents !
Et l'on assassinait chez toi impunément !

Gaules longues et fines, gaules qui battez cet arbre !
Vous sans lesquelles un fruit n'est jamais mûr !
brisez sur mon échine vos doigts crochus !

Faites

que mon visage vogue sur ces galets !

J'offre au ciel une couronne de scolopendres !
J'offre au ciel mon foie jaune et mes nuits calcinées !
A toi, j'offre ma tête sur le billot.

C'était son cœur qui vivait là, dans ces rocailles
entre ces nopals et ces euphorbes au lait jaunâtre...
dans ces épines et ces incendies d'été qui ne consumaient
que le roc, le quartz et la terre effarée du
labeur exsudé par les haines.

L'été faisait craquer sa chevelure... Ses pieds peints
au henné déshéritaient les fleurs et les abeilles. Les

perhaps a moon that will set its traps
with its tongue, blowing out our stars.
Dead? No! Worn out from a bittersweet,
unconsummated love…

The reeds were thrumming into wedding drums,
the dance of the men at the bottom of the well stained
in blood,
quicker than lightning, the young girl left my side.

Her small roseate belly in the clear waters of the river,
her small breasts, radiant as pomegranates…
her whole body washed away in one stream of blood.
This harmattan so beyond me! This windstorm! This inept tribe
of whirling demons!
And she was killed, right next to you, with impunity!

Saplings long and slender, saplings which beat against this tree!
Without whom no fruit would ever begin to ripen!
Whip your crooked fingers across my spine!

                          See to it

my face goes drifting away over these pebbles!

I offer the heavens a crown woven from scolopendra!
I offer the heavens my ycllow liver and my burnt-out nights!
And to you, I offer my head on a platter.

It was her heart that beat here once, amid this scree of stone,
amid the nopals and euphorbia, their yellowish milk…,
amid the thistles and blazing wildfires of summer
consuming nothing but rock, quartz, and soil, dismayed
by the lengths that hate will go to.

The summer used to make her hair shimmer… Her feet, painted
with henna, put the flowers and the bees both to shame. The

cigales interrompaient leur chant pour lui livrer passage.

La mort autour de moi hennissant qui récite
aux morts mes vies de ruine, pierre à pierre,
sous les grenadiers, par le torrent et sans prière
quand l'aube exhume mon corps et le délite.

J'abandonne mes rides à la vitre précaire
debout, vibrant, serpent debout autour
du sein dont la pointe a décroché le ciel,
ample chair aux clartés rageuses et pures.

cicadas would interrupt their song, simply to grant her safe passage.

Death, braying around me in every direction, shouting out the
names gone to ruin before me, under the pomegranate trees,
stone after stone after stone, next to the riverbed, bereft of
prayer, as dawn exhumes my body, and then disintegrates it.

I shed my shriveled skin in front of this precarious window—
upright, vibrant, an upright serpent, wrapping itself around
her breast, the end of which has brought down the heavens,
ample flesh bathing in the purest, most furious lucidity of it all.

LETTRE D'AMOUR AUX ANGES QUI N'ÉCOUTENT PAS

C'est du fond de l'hibiscus portant le monde sur
ses doigts
et nu jusqu'à la taille, l'arc tendu vers ta voix ;

c'est du fond de l'espace enfermé dans mes yeux,
sans papillon, sans rose, embué par tes yeux...
Ah ! c'est du fond d'un ciel crépusculaire

(Lamentable couché sur un banc de cérastes,
les dents rongées d'années-lumière) ;
c'est du fond des miroirs brisés que je te vois

naître en émulsion rouge et verte à travers
ce sahara fébrile...
Ici le bombyx fait éclater ses fils.

Ni la datte mûre, Soleil, c'est toi qui nargues
cette mer... ni le lait rance qui nous consume...
et ni la cavalcade qui détone sous tes nerfs,
cheval hennissant du sourire des quasars...
rien, ici, qui retienne à mes abots
tes doigts très purs, tes doigts irréparables !

Chemins jouxtant le Temps tracé
dans nos opprobres. Hommes courbés sortant
d'eux-mêmes... Je t'invite
au festin de leur charogne.
Apporte le thym, la soldanelle ! Apporte
ton rire...

A minuit sur mon crâne, tes rameaux rouges et noirs
et des poux ! Des poux d'ancêtres ricaneurs...
A minuit, la flûte, le fusil et la flèche

A LOVE LETTER TO THE ANGELS WHO AREN'T LISTENING

From the depths of the hibiscus flower bearing the world upon
its fingertips,
stripped from the waist down, its curvature reaching out in the direction of your voice;

From the depths of space locked behind my eyelids,
butterfly-less, rose-less, glazing over with the fog of your eyes...
Ah!, from the depths of the twilight-inflected sky

(pitiable, laid out across a bank of horned vipers,
whose teeth, light-years ago, were ground down);
from the depths of shattered mirrors, I watch you

spring to life in an emulsion of red and green, making your way across
this febrile Sahara...,
to this place, here, where threads go spewing from the bombyx mori.

Not the ripened date, O Sun, you who continuously taunt
this sea..., nor the rancid milk that's consuming us...,
nor the thundering cavalcade subsuming your nerves,
horse braying with the cracked grin of the quasars...
There is nothing, here, that might pry your dutifully pure
fingers, your irreparable fingers, from my hobbles!

Paths adjoining Time, outlined
by our opprobrium. Scoliosed men sliding out
of their skin..., I offer you
a feast in the form of their corpse.
Break out the thyme, the soldanella! Break out
in laughter...

At the stroke of midnight, upon my skull: your red and black boughs
and pestilence!, the pestilence of sniggering ancestors...
At the stroke of midnight, the flute, the rifle, and the arrow

et la colère et le silence et le gong sourd
tapissant ma mémoire de multiples viols.

Corps absent, mineur des corps qui brisent
sous tes orteils les peuples sanguinaires...
tisonnant dans ton œil un monde germant
sous le poids du désir, sous le poids des canopes,
toi qui ne ris et ne pleures et ne frappes.

Désert sur mon visage écaillé, ride aiguë
de mon âme sur le dos hersé des mers...
Soubresaut retenu par le fil de l'épeire...
J'avance dans la verve d'un cimetière,
orpailleur des ténèbres, maître des lunes frappées
à mort.

    *   *   *

DAKAR ET GORÉE

Alentour ce vol d'éperviers exhumant l'or
des mers
et nos artères tranchées au rythme clair
des vagues
par le bruissement féminin des kôras.

C'est le soir des mythes qui se lève
et c'est Dakar et c'est Gorée ensemble
houleux agitant mon cœur perdu.

Ici la lumière sanctifie mon suicide
quand le plasma des nuits rieuses
libère mon amour en gerbes d'éperviers.

Que la rue insuffle à mon sang vaste

and the wrath and the silence and the muted gong
upholstering my memory with violation's variations.

O absent body, O destroyer of bodies, crushing
the blood-soaked people underneath your feet...
stoking a world inside your eye, blossoming
beneath the weight of desire, the weight of canopic jars,
you who laugh not, and who weep not, and who do not retaliate.

The desert against my scale-covered face, the sharp wrinkle
of my soul upon the harrowed spine of the seas...,
the soubresaut restrained by the web the orb weaver spins...,
I charge ahead with the verve of a cemetery,
gold-digger of darkness, master of moons dealt a deadly
blow.

*   *   *

DAKAR AND GORÉE

Nearby this flock of sparrow hawks exhuming the gold
of seas
along with our arteries sliced into the waves'
rhythmic clarity
by the feminine murmuration of the koras.

This is the evening that myth rises from;
and this, the combined tempestuousness
of Dakar and Gorée, stirring my forlorn heart.

Here, while the laughing plasma of night
releases my love into bouquets of sparrow hawks,
the light sanctifies my suicide.

May the street breathe something other than

à l'image saillante du basalte
un sourire autre que l'éclipse !

Je tanne ma peau d'éclairs, ô vieux
lions debout
face à la mer fourbue.

Que le baobab, que le tam-tam
du troglodyte fugueur
dansent en mon œil noyé du lait des mères !

*   *   *

À LÉOPOLD SÉDAR SENGHOR

C'est toute la nuit que le Fouta dresse
autour des choses et même
dans les élytres des insectes...
Une Casamance noueuse en ses bolongs et seule
mandingue jusqu'au cou
des dieux qui se délitent en ce musée superbe :
une nuit délicate tombée en mes paumes avec
ses étoiles en pirogues portées par toutes mes rides...

C'est l'aube d'hématine pourvoyant dans mes artères
et dans mes yeux si loin de ton visage
ton cœur aimé, roulé sur mes joues lorsque la mer
appelle.
Brise ! Ah ! brise ce cœur
comme un bol plein de sang que le sorcier inepte
oublie dans les trous magnifiques des songes !

Seul avec ma lampe et toi si proche battant à mes
tempes
doucement...

the grin of eclipses into the vastness of my blood,
via the salient image of basalt!

I tan my lightning-strike of a skin, O lions
of old, O over-
seers of sea-weariness.

May the baobab, may the tam-tam
of the fugitive troglodyte
overflowing with mother's milk, dance inside my eye!

*   *   *

FOR LÉOPOLD SÉDAR SENGHOR

It's the night's entirety that the Futa Tooro looms up
and around all things, even
the insects' elytra...
A Casamancean woman entangled in its bolong trees and a lone
Mandinka man up to the neck
in gods crumbling into this one superb museum:
such a delicate night dropped into my palms, with
its pirogue-like stars carried upon the surface of my wrinkles...

It's the hematite dawn flooding my arteries
and my eyes, so far away from your face,
your beloved heart, rolling over my cheeks as the sea
calls out.
Break it! Ah! Break open this heart,
like some vessel flooded with blood, left behind by some inept
sorcerer in the magnificent, dreamy trenches!

Alone with you and my lamp; you so close that I can feel you beat against
my temples
ever so gently...

ton corps vaste, impalpable occupant l'appartement
je te vois. Je vois danser l'indicible ; je caresse
ton petit secret que pas une orchidée ne peut ravir,
devant la baie ouverte
et la bière fumant dans son verre et la terre
exhalant un jour lourd, exhalant des corbeaux.

Papayer lancé au vent et que le criquet charge
d'un message amoureux où le ciel s'illumine,
nous voici réunis sur tes palmes adverses.
Ah ! que s'éloigne enfin le boa et que vienne
le son danseur !

Ancêtres bâtisseurs d'empires, grands querelleurs
Femmes du Sud qui tailladiez mon front,
et toi, poète assis le goulot à la bouche
sur une place de Marrakech ou de Séville...
j'apporte un hivernage rythmé par le frisson
de la nuit des bolongs et des palétuviers.

your vast, impalpable body fleshing out the apartment,
I see you. I see the inexpressible perform its dance; I caress
your little secret that no orchid shall ever ravish,
before the wide-open bay
and the beer foaming over the rim of its glass, and the earth
breathing out the day's weight, breathing out the blackness of the crows.

The papaya tree whirling in the wind; this, the cricket shall inscribe
with a tender-loving message for the heavens to illuminate;
here we are, reunited over your adverse palm leaves.
Ah!, may the boa relinquish its grip at last, and may we usher in
the dancing sound!

Ancestors, empire-builders, great quarreling tribes!
Women of the South who hack their way into my forehead,
and you, poet, who lean back, your lips around the bottle,
out and about in some square, in Marrakesh or Seville…
I bring about a rhythmic overwintering, one that will travel the shiver
down the mangrove and the bolong trees, by way of night.

CÉRÉMONIAL DE COUPURES NÈGRES

Que d'aucuns giclant de ma pierre rident ta peau
marécage
sans faille portant très haut le monde atroce !
Les roches, les serpents dans la nuit se souviennent,
homme inepte t'en allant par-delà l'écurie !
il arrache serpolet, il arrache colliers d'astres
par cette nuit sans plume édifiée sur ton affre,
brigand qui enroules en ta poche mon chemin !

Tous jouent, oui, tous se sucrent
sauvages !
Alentour du roc, alentour du corail...
équarrissent ta larme, t'extirpent du sol,
séquoia ; te tuent, Indien ; ils mangent
et se vautrent et se roulent et se suicident.

Mon front énorme, mon front, oublie l'araire !

THE RITUALISTIC SLASHING OF NEGROS

May some spewing from my stone shrivel your fleshy,
flawless
quagmire, and hoist this atrocious world into the air!
Every rock, every nocturnal serpent moving through the night will remember,
foolhardy man, how you made your way out of the stable!
Clawing the thyme, clawing the collars of celestial bodies,
in the featherless night alighted by your woe,
O brigand, you who roll my path up into your pocket!

Everyone plays along, yes, everyone lines their pockets,
those savages!
Rounding the rock, rounding the coral…,
skinning your teardrop, uprooting you from soil,
sequoia; slaughtering you, Indian; they devour you,
wallow about, roll around, lay themselves to waste.

My brow, my enormous brow, wipe your mind of the swing plow!

ARAIRE

Quand le sel de mer vu et revu
judicieusement par la ruine de ta langue —
cœurs ouverts aux iules absentes —
quand le fumier dont ta vie se repaît
quand la femme et son cortège de lithobies
par ces ruelles où ruisselle le délire
— crânes éclatés contre les murs, couteaux que tire
le silence gavé du rire
de ta tête qui ne garde de moi que mon éclair !...

Quand la ville obstrue le ciel avec les tripes
et le vomi d'enfants tués
sur l'ictère de ton sourire —
faste !
quand je réprime ta peur
avec une virgule d'où suinte ton sang aigre !...

Quand le pays fabrique sa mort, debout
sur lui seul en guêpes grenadières...
quand l'orage dicte sa loi à la théière...
quand les puits puent, quand les najas
boivent l'œil des mères...

Le Sud éclate en mille rapières
ébouriffant tes nerfs...
et l'araire jubile sur la pierre plate où erre
un peuple pendu aux étoiles délétères.

Ce peuple là, tu le connais ? Non ! Tu l'as
seulement entrevu renversé par une auto.
Une femme, mince et belle, regardait mourir
l'ouvrier... Ses mollets bruns et saillants
à contre-jour sur le sang

SWING PLOW

The moment the salt of the envisioned sea returns
judiciously re-envisioned along the ruinousness of your tongue—
hearts opening into absent julidae—
The moment your life worms through its fertilizer,
The moment woman and her entourage of lithobiidae
follow these throughways, thoroughly delirious
—skulls smashed to smithereens against the walls, knives drawn
from the sheath of silence, choking through the laughter
of your head filled with nothing but my lightning!...

The moment the city obstructs the sky with the intestines
and vomit of hanged children,
swaying from the icterus of your smile—
how wondrous!
The moment I whip back your fear
with a comma of your caustic blood, come oozing!...

The moment the country conjures an industry of death, looming
over it, with the single mind of pomegranate wasps...,
the moment the storm lays down the law to the teapot...
the moment the wells go putrid, the moment cobras
swallow motherly eyes...

The South explodes into a thousand rapiers
disheveling your every nerve...,
and the swing plow reigns over the doldrums of stone people
wandering about, suspended from the stars, disintegrating.

These people, do you even recognize them? No!, you've only caught
glimmers of them sucked under the wheel of passing cars.
A woman, slender and beautiful, looked on
as the working man drew his last breath...His sunbaked, shapely calves
contrasted sharply against the blood

qui coulait sur la chaussée. L'auto brillait
au soleil de quatre heures.

*　　　*　　　*

L'enfant du riche s'amusait avec la boue du torrent.
Il était content. Tout l'été houspillait son petit corps doré.

*　　　*　　　*

L'enfant du pauvre, qui n'a jamais franchi la montagne,
chantait et taillait des roseaux. Il barbotait et pêchait
tranquillement. Il était puni.

*　　　*　　　*

Celle que tu aimes est porteuse de girofles
et de clous et de bagues et de rire nocturnes ;
un torrent de cailloux roule dans ses yeux clairs :
elle est l'habit indispensable du jour.

Je sais que ta licence glissait, femme nue, sur toi...
au bord des vagues claquait en méduses obèses.
Je sais que le Temps existe,
coiffé de sabres, assis sur la peau de peuples amers.
Et ce morveux qui rutile sur ton saccage,
ô mère !

Les serpents, les scorpions, les rats eux-mêmes,
tous bavaient, caressaient mes plaies humides.

On agitait mon sort sous la meule, on écrasait
une orge pétillante.
Et les femmes chantaient. Un vieux lépreux disait
sa mémoire à la route : "Il n'y a rien au-delà de
cette montagne"

Plus tard, je découvris le monde tel qu'il est.

flowing out and onto the highway. The car, it twinkled
in the afternoon sun.

*　　　*　　　*

The rich man's child was playing around in the torrent's mud. He was full of joy.
The entirety of summer was upbraiding his blissful little body.

*　　　*　　　*

The poor man's child, who never made his way to the other side of the mountain, was singing and sharpening reeds. He was paddling and fishing peacefully.
He was punished.

*　　　*　　　*

The one you love is the bearer of cloves,
nails, rings, and nocturnal laughter;
a torrent of gravel rolls around inside her enlightened eyes:
for she is the indispensable vestment of day.

Naked woman, I know that your licentious ways would swim over you…
on the verge of waves, slapping like obese jellyfish.
I know that Time exists,
coiffed with swords, lounging across the skin of an embittered people.
And this little twerp shining out over your devastation,
O mother!

The serpents, the scorpion, the rats themselves
all foamed at the mouth, grazing my freshly opened wounds.

My destiny writhed beneath the grinding wheel; a vibrant grain
of barley, to be crushed.
And the women would sing. An old leper along the road
would speak his truth: "there is nothing beyond
that mountain"

Later, I discovered the world as it is.

LA BELLE RIVIÈRE

L'été cassé sur ta tête, consommé
en timbales de glaise sèche — l'été
répudié à coup de thé, très réprimé,
hurlant par mes pores toute sanie.

Cette gorgée d'eau que chaque grain
d'or évapore, c'est le vieux rêve
du sedentaire et de l'errant...

Elle est sèche la belle rivière où tes lèvres
gouvernaient mes pieds fendus, sont secs tes seins
la belle rivière couronnée de sangsues.

THIS BEAUTIFUL RIVER

The summertime broken over your head, consumed
by the drums of the dried-out clay—the summertime
abandoned for sips of tea, remarkably restrained,
screaming through every last of my festering pores.

This mouthful of water that every golden seedling
evaporates into thin air, such is the old dream
of the sedentary, and the wanderers…

It's gone dry now, this beautiful river, where your lips
once guided my splitting feet, dry as your breasts,
this beautiful river, crowned with leeches.

MARGELLE

Qui dit cercle dit cerceau ! Es-tu si simple, tête ?
oh ma tête ! es-tu encore sauvage ?

Tes guenilles, soleil, ton poudroiement, miroir
rompu ! Rendu grain à grain sur le pavé !

Ils agitent mon nerf giclé d'ors fins, jubilent
sur les drapeaux.

Dans l'oubliette, sur le radoub, dans l'incomplet grimoire,
dans l'or ! Terreur ! dans l'or en geysers putréfiants !

Fille ! ô fillette depuis longtemps noyée
quand l'oued surgissant roidement de son tonnerre,
sans égard pour ton corps,
emmêla ton sang aux filiformes racines.

COPING

What means of circle is a circling means! Are you that simple, head?
Oh my head! Are you still wild?

Your tattered rags, O sun, your shimmery gleam, a shattered
mirror!, rendered grain-by-grain into the pavement!

They make my nerves writhe, gushing with golden finery, gloating
over the flags.

Inside oblivion itself, out on the dry-dock, inside the unfinished grimoire,
inside the gold! Terror! Inside the gold, inside the putrefying geysers!

You, just a girl! O a little girl, long ago drowned,
as the wadi, rising sharply out of its thunderstorms,
without a thought to your body,
entangled your blood in its spindly roots.

LABOUR A KAN

à Jean-Marie Domenach

Toujours l'enfance amère retournée dépecée
sur les soieries du labour et du chant,
hésitante mais sautillant entre mes doigts
sur les cupules où le rêve me foudroie.

De quelle menace narguer le dard acerbe
et le tordre le tordre contre les cloisons
de la nuit épouvantable qui désherbe
ce pays au fond de tes yeux comme un poison ?

Le vent brise ses pupitres sur tes cils,
les forêts d'arganiers déterrent la hache,
la tornade noue sa chevelure
à tes chevilles à ton cou de totem.

Nuit sanglante enflée du rire ruffian !
Combien de têtes roulent dans ce délire ?
Combien de cœurs fragiles de sexes durs broyés
sur l'arène sur la corne allumée au zénith ?

Mais toujours l'enfance sécrète l'or lapidaire,
engoncée dans les ailes-couperets de l'exil ;
je lis sur ses lèvres l'ondoiement funéraire
du mur-huant qui ricoche sur ton pistil.

Il y eut des printemps âpres ; les jeunes seins
des mères flottaient à la dérive...
les aigles d'en haut nous jetaient le sommeil :
l'amandier, l'amandier blanc captait la mort.

Heures égrenés avec le corset des termites,
terre essoufflée juchée en rire suant
sur le corps des trilobites,
fusils au bout d'une pierre me huant !

PLOWING IN KAN

for Jean-Marie Domenach

Forever that bitter childhood returning, churning
over the laborious and song-filled silk factories,
hesitating, before shooting through my fingers
into my cupula, where the dream like lightning strikes.

What threat is mocking that acrimonious sting,
this writhing, writhing against the cloisters
of night's colossal shroud, pulling this country's
weeds up like poison through your bottomless eyes?

The wind splits school-desks across your eyelashes,
forests of argan trees exhume the axe,
a tornado knots its hair
to your ankles, to your neck's totem.

The blood-soaked night is swollen with vagrant laughter!
How many heads go whirling into that delirium?
How many fragile hearts, how many fossilized genitalia are impaled
upon the horn, inside this arena, illuminated at its zenith?

But childhood goes on and on, secreting its lapidary gold,
sinking beneath the cleaver-wings of exile;
on its lips, I can just make out the funerary undulations
of a shriek-wall ricocheting from your pistil.

There were some crueler springtimes; the young breasts
of mothers floating upon the breeze...
from up on high, eagles would throw down dreams for us:
almond trees, white almond trees, grasping at death.

The hours were threshed with the corset of termites;
a breathless land, laughter looming above and then oozing
down, onto the body of the trilobites—
firearms dotting the surface of the rocks, shrieking!

MOI DEBOUT SUR LA TERRASSE

Ce sommeil... Moi debout sur la terrasse
voyant au loin des corps giclés des pierres
remuant dans la boue âcre qui te scelle
au sol et au sel, mère que je ne vois pas,
subreptice, coulée sous l'ourlet du songe amer

Je m'accoude au muret ; la fête bat
le tonnerre sur les nattes, sur les plis
épars et forts, sur le ciel, sur tes yeux : l'or
habille ma voix de vallées sciées d'opprobre
et d'îlots arrachés aux fêtes précaires
balayeuses d'ailes de ramier sur le muret.

Satyre inepte suant sur la femme du mort
enfermé dans le gosier tortueux du corbeau !
Hilare, surinant le blé, tailladant l'orge !
Du puits, oui, du puits, tu tires ton lait !

AS I STEP OUT ONTO THE TERRACE

This sleep-like state...As I step out onto the terrace
watching from afar as the stones spew bodies,
writhing through the odious mud sealing you
into the soil and salt, surreptitious mother,
cast beneath the dream's bitter hem, who I can't see

I lean forward over the balcony; the festivals reverberate
thunderously over every last mat, every last crease,
strewn and strident; over the sky, over your eyes: the gold
swathes my voice in the sawed-out valleys of shame
and small islands torn from uneasy festivals
sweeping like the wings of pigeons over the low-rising wall.

An inept satyr drooling over the wife of the dead man
locked deep down inside the raven's tortuous throat!
Maniacal laughter, slashing through the wheat, the barley!
Deep inside the wells, yes, the wells you draw your milk from!

POIDS & MESURES

Tout ce qui se salit, chien, toute engeance en toi
broie et troue ce siècle à coups
de faux sur l'envers des clepsydres du grimoire.

Alentour le dhole roué d'astres termité
dévide cette nue de chaînes d'abots et d'aigres
sangs
en colère minutée par tes sauts d'homme muré...

quelle montée prendre ici
quand d'aucuns dansent que tous s'excitent
à ras des peaux tendues sur l'éclair sur le fil
des cimeterres jetés entre ton œil et moi ?

Ciel du matin rouge d'éclats ruant, séides
soûlés de lymphe, buvez donc
ce sang ! Et toi, vieux chien,
endosse l'effraction des sites, lacère mes rides !

WEIGHTS AND MEASURES

All who roll in their own filth, fleabag, every spawn engendering you
grinds into, digs away at this century with
its scythes, opposing the grimoire's clepsydra.

All around the dhol reeling with termite-eaten stars
the starkness of the kick-chains and the blood comes unwound,
curdling
into a rage amassed minute-to-minute by the immured leaps of mankind...

what ascension can proceed here
while out there, they dance and dance, everyone's flesh growing
flush with ecstasy, stretched across the lightning, across the strung-out
cemeteries cast before your eye, before my own?

Red sky of morning gone wild with explosions, Seids who drink
themselves drunk on lymphatic fluid, bring the blood
to your lips! And as for you, you old fleabag,
embrace this invasion, slice open my shriveled flesh!

CORVÉE D'ATTA
à Paul Thibaud

Sur mon corps la ville pose ses cataclysmes —
eux gavés ne mourant de rien — quand ce sicaire
lâche sur toi la meute
je redéterre l'amulette
qui gâche ma nuit somptuaire :
têtes éclaboussements murs corps dits aux mots saignés
sur l'asphalte et peut-être
peut-être une ruée de planètes !
sur mon corps la ville pose ses cataclysmes.

Ce peuple assis sur des tornades, Soleil !
larmes et sang coliques, colères des sables :
nuées d'opprobre et d'enfants psalmodiant
battus sur l'étoile d'un ciel truand ;
la poussière de tes yeux, mère,
scindée en rêves, en mantes noires,
les bâtons, les tessons qui font couronne
et péril autour de toi ; l'or qui saccage
ce peuple assis sur des tornades, Soleil !

Pourriture installée creusant plasma brisant
les peuples sans ce peuple abouti au désastre
l'enfance s'arme d'un astre tanguant
entre moi tendu comme la corde du cambri
dans ces villes ni plus vivantes qu'un forficule
se riant de tes lobes, de tes yeux qui se noient
ni moins mortes que la pierre rêche des tablettes
inexhumables — Sijilmassa Ifni Anoual —
pourriture installée creusant plasma brisant.

Il joue sous le tilleul et nargue les masques
qui lacèrent mes peaux de lycaon

THE WEARINESS OF ATTA
for Paul Thibaud

The cataclysms of the city cast themselves over my body—
the ones who, force-fed, are dying of nothing—when the Sicarii
release their hounds
on you, again I find myself unearthing what precious charm
I might squander my luxurious night with:
skulls, bespatterings, walls, bodies expressed in blood-soaked words
over the asphalt, and maybe,
just maybe, an onslaught of planets!
The cataclysms of the city cast themselves over my body.

This people seated upon a sum of tornados, O Sun!
tears and blood-colored colic, wrathful sands:
stripped of disgrace and children, swollen with song,
beaten against the star of delinquent heavens;
the dust of your eyes, O mother,
bisected into dreams, into black mantises,
switches, tesserae, surrounding you
with crown and peril; the gold that lays waste
This people seated upon a sum of tornados, O Sun!

A built-in putrefaction rifling through the plasma breaking down
the people on the outskirts of The People bound for disaster
the years of youth arming themselves with a star pitching back
and forth before my I arrives stretched out like a gambri string
across these cities looking no livelier than your average earwig
laughing through your earlobes, through your drowned-out eyes
no unlivelier than the coarseness of stone over the inexhumable
slabs of stone—Sijilmassa, Ifni, Anoual—
A built-in putrefaction rifling through the plasma breaking down.

Under the lime tree, making a game of it, he mocks the masquerades
doing their best to carve out my lycanthropic flesh

en mille rires ébouriffés.
Les femmes dansent sur la vallée, mes nerfs extirpent
le torrent, mes nerfs me hissent

loin, très loin au-dessus de vos banques,
au-dessus des rampements, au-dessus des maléfices :
corvée d'Atta et cloportes et carabes.
Il joue sous le tilleul et nargue les masques !

into one thousand slovenly sneers.
Women dance throughout the valley, my nerves uproot
the torrent, my nerves lift me up

and far away, very far away, high up beyond your riverbanks,
high up beyond the mountain tops, high up beyond the malfeasance:
the weariness of Atta and the woodlice and the scarabs.
Under the lime tree, making a game of it, he mocks the masquerades!

RIVIÈRE, SEL ET TERREURS

Ceux qui portent des bijoux ou celles qui portent
des fleurs.
Tête ! O tête incommensurablement ruinée,
fendue en élytres déterrés par ma mémoire...
et du pays agitant l'or, la noire
route et les puits en ciguë fleurissant...

Ceux qui par moi vivent, ne vivent pas, qui tuent
sans grade, suintant sur la terre, sur la rivière,
sur tes frères, sur la mort, sur la ville, sur tes yeux...
fille, va-t-en ! le chemin perd ses plumes, la piste,
de jour en jour, se change en grosses vipères.

Une fille superbe éradiquant le rire,
sortie de toi seul en masse outrecuidante,
par la ténèbre s'en va vers tes rides, vers la précaire
bouche qui ne consume absolument qu'un homme.

Debout vous autres ! Vous qui n'êtes que le sourire
de vagues en allée sous la feuillée, de vagues
écrasées sous le rostre ! Est-ce que je suis l'abeille ?
La belle abeille sinon la guêpe suante...
Tu le dis, vieux poltron, vieux chien, tu le dis, Rire.

Les putes amarrées aux mâles et aux poings,
cherchant sous le grain de ma peau 'atroce vertu ;
toi morte, jetée peut-être mal brûlée !
oiseau mieux qu'un homme, toi, fillette en délire,
raide lorsque ta prise mon doigt en involucre,
plus belle justement alors même que la mort
succincte, sous ces arbres et ces terreurs couchées,
sabote l'éclat des ailes qui bruissent en ton sang
avec ce cortège, avec ces rêves sanglés,
m'oxygénant atrocement, répudiant de ma rétine
l'ombre et l'éclair d'ombres abouties au soleil.

RIVER, SALT, AND TERRORS

Those who bring about jewels or those who bring about
flowers.
Head! O head, immeasurably ruined,
split into elytra, unearthed via my memory…
emerging from this country brandishing its gold, its shadowy
highways, and its wells laced with hemlock flowers…

Those living who surround me are not alive, those murderers,
unworthy of their rank, go slithering out over the earth, over the river,
over your brothers, over death, over this city, over your eyes…
run, little girl! Feathers flee this course of flight, with every
passing day, the winding road unfurls into corpulent vipers.

A breathtaking girl breaking through the absurdity
emerges from within you in one overweened mass
via the obscurity, your shriveled skin, your precarious
mouth consuming no more than a man, albeit absolutely.

All you others, rise up! You who are but the sweeping smile
of the waves, swept beneath the foliage, of the waves
breaking against the rostrum! Am I a bee?
The gorgeous bee, or else or some drooping wasp…
Say it old coward, you lowlife, go ahead and say it, O Laughter.

The whores all moored to the array of phalluses and fists,
searching my folds of peeled-back flesh for some atrocious virtue;
you, dead, thrown out perhaps, crudely consumed by fire!
Man, outdone by a bird, and you, a delirious young girl,
completely still as you wrapped your hand around my finger like a husk,
more beautiful in that moment than at the moment of
your demise, under these trees and their terrors lying in wait,
the eruption of wings funneling their noise through your blood,
alongside this procession, alongside these drawn-back dreams,
forcing the air atrociously into my lungs, spitting from my eye
obscurity and obscurity's illumination, both ending in sunlight.

45

TERRE, PLUMEAUX & LUNE

Toutes les pierres dévident autour de toi mon corps.
Toute la terre se soulève ! Le ciel éclate ;
en des sanies hurlantes qui baignent
ce soleil concassé sur mon dos comme un galet.

L'été éclatant affleure à tes yeux noirs
et le sable sonne l'heure exiguë où je contemple
ton œil vertical oublié sous les décombres
de ma nuit abattue par le rire du caracal.

Sur la place les hommes négocient le sang des morts
et les mémoires en éboulis et tes lèvres de rivière
sous ton effigie répudiée, ô Soleil !
réprimé à coup de thé et de timbales vermeilles.

Quand la lune dans mon sang agite ses plumeaux
d'autres prennent la charrue et les drapeaux brûlés :
Harlem ! Mon cher Harlem ! toi qui ne parles pas !
Oiseau bondissant sur moi, me tuant net.

Et nous, contigus sous les figuiers patients !
Seins d'hyènes, mamelles de lycaons
ruant d'ichneumons tresseurs de têtes —
vieille étoile repue des scories de villes tuées.

Elle nargue l'Absent, l'écheveau autoritaire :
filet de cordes dont le blé et les cadavres
défont les spires en fumées flamboyantes
sur un peuple gémissant, se tenant la rate amère

Lui courant à l'envi sur le rostre, teignant
l'ongle faste que ciel et terre soudoient...
Tes paupières en dérive vers l'erratique soleil
non sanglé fuyant l'opprobre qui nous ceint !

EARTH, FEATHERY PLUMES, AND MOON

O my body, all the stones are coming undone around you.
All the earth is rising! The sky, flashing;
screaming out in wounds, bathing
this sun throttling its way down my spine like a scree-ridden slope.

The dazzling summer runs flush with your blacked-out eyes,
and the sands sound the exiguous hour as I contemplate
your eye's verticality, lost to the ruins
of my night, encircled by the laughter of caracals.

Throughout the square, men deal in the blood of the dead
and the memorials lost to landslides and your rivering lips
under your repudiated effigy, O Sun!
Repressed into rounds of tea and vermillion drumbeats.

When my lunar blood goes writhing into its feathery plumes,
others take up plow blades and burnt flags:
Harlem! My dear Harlem! You whose words escape you!
Bird unbound above me, bringing me swift death.

You and I, we are contiguous beneath the patience of the fig trees!
The breasts of hyenas, the teats of wild lycaons,
swarming with head-spinning ichneumons—
one well-aged astral body, sated by the sight of slain cities.

It mocks the Absent One, that authoritarian skein:
an entwining mesh whose wheat and corpses
unspool into spires of vibrant smoke-rings
over a people, wailing, clutching their putrid spleens!

A people coursing ad infinitum across the rostrum, dying
the lavishly-hued fingernail corrupted by heaven and earth…
Your eyelids gone drifting toward the erratic, unbound
sunlight, fleeing the opprobrium that closes in around us!

Ecrasé ou riant, souriant ou surinant,
homme non écrit, toujours inepte et sûr
du bras séculier qui détériore le socle
dans le fourmillement des étoiles délétères.

Crushed-out or exploding in laughter, lashing inward
or outward; man, unspoken, ever-artless, ever-assured
of the secular arm slowly wearing away the pedestal
via the tingling sensation of the stars' disintegration.

A BOUT PORTANT

Alentour ce vol de cicindèles, toi blottie
au fond d'un rêve ceint de cobalt,
de ciels aptes et d'écumes sur quoi trotte
mon âme amerrie en tes yeux. Autour de toi,
cette mer âcre qui délire
en échos de peuples abattus dans les rues !
Mon cœur exsangue effeuille le sort
des hommes calleux fusillés à bout portant.

Sont-ce des tueurs ? Non ! Des lâches ! Ce sont
des lâches
qui consument ton corps
et s'y lovent ! Peuple, ce sont
tes chromosomes infects qui tuent !

Soleil ! Terre ! Garrigue ! Port ! Soleil !
Je m'arme ! Mes nerfs s'infestent de scorpions
délicieux autant que le sang d'un Arabe
bu sous la vigne atroce de mon père.
Soleil ! Terre ! Port gluant ! Soleil, tu pues !

Et s'ils t'atterrent, mon cœur comblé de morgues
à l'orée du nuage réfractaire ?
Si la terre tout entière qu'exhausse ton cadavre
m'adjoint l'aube héréditaire —
fourbu, rotules percées par des mirages puissants ?

Assise au bord des lèvres ouvertes au songe
sur un sofa d'abeilles précaires
et doucement bercée, encombrée par les vents,
répudiée, morte, grimée sur ce ciel térébrant !
Mère, je t'écoute et suspends à tes yeux
ces breloques qui heurtent mon sang !

AT POINT-BLANK RANGE

Somewhere in this swarm of cicindelas you appear, nestled
deep inside your own dreams, girded by cobalt,
heavenly views, and foam upon which my sea-
wracked soul runs into your eyes. Around you, all around you,
the sharpness of the sea whirls
into the echoes of a people beaten senseless in the streets!
My bloodless heart goes sailing the destiny
of hardened men, shot through the head, at point-blank range.

Are these murderers? No! Cowards! These are
cowards
who consume your body
and curl up inside! People, these are
your own infected chromosomes that kill!

Sun! Earth! Garrigue! Harbor! Sun!
I am taking up arms! My nerves swarming with scorpions
delicious as an Arab's blood
guzzled in my father's atrocious vineyard.
Sun! Earth! Viscous harbor! Sun, you have gone to rot!

And does that appall you, O heart, overflowing with morgues
on the outskirts of the refractory cloud?
What if the entirety of earth lifting your corpse sky-high
were to adjoin me to dawn, passed-down—
worn out, ball-joints pierced by the overwhelming mirages?

Dangling from the end of lips opening into a dream,
onto a sofa of indelicate bees,
weighed down, swishing gently through the breeze,
disowned, deathly, and gummed up in the ear-splitting sky!
I hear you, O mother, and from your eyes I suspend
these breloques hurtling through my blood!

OUED ET SANG

Le sang sourd de toi, oued, le sang sertit
de phosphore et d'or ce reg
rompu sur mon échine ivre de balles.

Oriflammes, tôles rouillées, chair tordue
sans cercueil, sans canope, torrent sec
où la larme de la femme tourbillonne

fraîche éclose, geôlière incongrue du soleil.

Les hommes sont d'argile forte et d'orge froide,
leurs os saillent du galet roide,
éclairs qui musellent l'œil, dans sur le fil
fin des dagues.

Mère lacérée, oued acerbe !
Terre étouffée, ciel putrescible !
Orpailleuse qui me vêts du lait noir de la tribu !

Violette, les autres fuyant devant,
déclouant du sol, des nues les étoiles, les palmiers,
jetant aux hyènes ma face, mes tripes, mon sang
lorsqu'ils descellent les pierres brutes de ma raison!

Si subitement que du sable monte le chant
grégaire
sans timbre, soufflant dans l'infini étroit...

Chevauchées, torsions, corps suants, vieilles clameurs,
sauts de fonte, scintillement des sabres
sur le poudroiement des corolles, sur l'hysope,
sur le haje, sur la femme, sur la Lune.

WADI AND BLOOD

There is a blood that spews out of you, wadi, blood swirling
with phosphor and gold, this reg
broken against my intoxicated bandolier of a spine.

Oriflammes, rusted sheets of metal, contorted flesh
with no coffin, with no canopic jar, a dry torrent
into which the freshly eclosed tears of women,

each one the sun's unseemly jailer, go whirling.

The men retain an air of robust clay and cold barley,
their bones protrude from the hardened stone,
flashes of lightning muzzle the eye, dancing across the fine
edge of daggers.

Utterly mauled, this mother; a wadi grown acidic!
Smothered earth; compostable sky!
Gold miner swaddling me in the tribe's blackened milk!

A violet glow, and some others running ahead of me:
wrenching nails from the soil, the stripped stars, the palm trees,
leaving my face, my entrails, and my blood to the hyenas,
as they continue to work the last crude stone of my reason loose!

Abruptly: so abruptly that the sands rupture, and a gregarious,
timbre-less
song arises, blowing through infinity's pass…

The chevauchées, the torsions, the sweaty corpses,
the leaps of smelting fumes, the scintillation of sabers
across the glimmering corollas, across the hyssop,
across the haje, across woman, across the Moon.

Lisant ta genèse dans une datte trop mûre,
en cercle autour du feu bleu terrasseur,
roi des troupeaux, roi des socles en scories,
Archonte des villes de pisé arc-boutées
sur les séismes qui rident le sang remis...

Les masques, les ferrements, les hontes tomberont,
charriés par le métal
du Sud conscrit s'étreignant la poitrine...
les palais englués dans leur lymphe craqueront
sur ta tête, impassible auteur du vent ancien.

And reading your genesis from an overripened date,
in a circle around the blue of these wilting flames,
is the king of the herds, the king of devastated pedestals,
the Archon of cities, of rammed earth bracing themselves
for a series of seismic waves that will wrinkle a blood repaid...

The masques, the shackles, the sheer shame of it all: everything shall fall,
everything shall be swept downstream by the South's
compulsions, arms folded across the chest...,
and the palaces, mired in their lymph, shall crack open
over your head, O impassible author of ancient wind.

PÉLAGIQUE

Il n'y a plus, mon cœur, qu'à en découdre avec
la pélagique cohorte qui détruit le polyptère ;
tes cils l'ont savamment enrobé de boue craquée.
Il n'y a plus ici qu'un hoquet délétère.

Les barques sont brûlées ! Arrière ver apte, coquilles,
colifichets tintant sur la bosse du dromadaire !
Que ce vent s'encrapule et herse de typhons
et déride ta face en crampe sur mes béquilles !

L'astre dur écrasa la ténèbre tutélaire
et la verte algue et la grêle qui grime ma terre
radiant du puits pur l'hirondelle, le tonnerre
et l'eau — Qu'en est-il de cette eau mercurielle ?

Ils entassent des fastes, des chiffres sur les protons,
d'une pichenette envoient dinguer le prolétaire ;
ils tirent du matin jusqu'au soir sur les fils
qui t'encombrent, océan belliqueux mais très précaire.
Et quand ils voient la femme, leurs élytres se froissent
et crissent sur le fer oxydé par ta mémoire ;
ils s'affolent et blasphèment l'indestructible grimoire
pour un peu d'or volé au feu qui t'amenuise.

Ils assassinent avec tes mains, éboulent ta chair
tombée sur ma taie en âpre rutilance...
Contre eux, tout s'insurge : le cancrelat, l'aster
et l'abeille porteuse d'étoiles alphabétiques.

PELAGIC

O my heart, there is nothing left, only to confront, once and
for all, the pelagic horde that lets the dragonfish languish;
your lashes, in their wisdom, have smoothed it over with cracked mud.
There is nothing left there, only one last noxious hiccup.

The ships have all been burned! The able worm left behind, along with shells,
with ornamental trinkets jingling against a camel's hump!
May this wind engulf itself, and may it unleash a series of typhoons,
may it smooth the wrinkles from your face, contorted against my crutches!

The star grew more steadfast, crushing the tutelary darkness,
the green algae, and the hailstones that grime up my land,
swallows, thunders, and waters radiating from the purest
of wells—what is it about that water, that mercurial water?

They can pile wonder on wonder, numbers upon protons,
and yet with a flick of their fingers, still send the proletariat flying;
From day to day, and night to night, they open fire on those
cumbersome few: a boisterous, though unpredictable ocean.
And when they see a woman somewhere, their elytra shrivel,
squeal against the iron-ore, oxidized by your memory;
they panic and blather their blasphemies against the indestructible grimoire
for one iota of gold, snatched from the flames disposing of your body.

They use your own hands to assassinate you, bringing your lowly flesh
down to the stinging glow of my pillowcase…
To them, everything is an insurgent: the cockroach, the aster,
and the bee, the bringer of alphabetical stars.

QUETZALCOATL

Dors ! Dors ! Sauvage ! Irascible sauvage
chancelant, tonsure au vent. Dors !
Il suffit qu'une mer, il suffit qu'une terre
te porte au-delà du ciel rieur
pour qu'éclatent l'or, le sang,
le sang grégaire, le sang opératoire.

Assis dans l'oponce, ruminant cette terreur,
face au tertre écroulé, face à l'acte éprouvant,
coeurs et carcans ceignant ton ombre amère...
Dors ! Sauvage ! En toi s'éveille la Tribu.

Il ensanglante l'arbre, il déterre l'inepte mémoire
suée, salie sur les yeux des vigognes...
Je la farde de déserts, de torches, d'enfants
morts sous le rire des turbans.

Là-haut dort le père, là-haut m'attend
l'étoile fascinée par mes sourires ;
masques et carcasses d'astres en suaire
qui de ce corps arrachent les clous tordus.

Ce tertre exhibe nos terreurs, fouillis
de vieux désastres inscrits dans ma rétine ;
j'arpente l'orage factieux, je te supprime !

Je voyage à travers les écailles et les frissons
du serpent. Et je couche dans l'insecte, j'écoute
penser les nombres.

QUETZALCOATL

Sleep on! Sleep on! Savage! You irascible, faltering
savage, you tonsure of the wind. Sleep on!
It's enough that one sea, enough that one earth,
buoys you forth, beyond heavenly laughter,
ensuring what shines on: that gold, that blood,
that co-mingling blood, that surgical blood.

Nestled atop the prickly pear, brooding over this terror,
before the bowled-over tomb, before the chaotic deed,
hearts and heartless shackles encircling your bitter shadow…
Sleep on! Savage! Sleep on! Inside you looms the Tribe.

He steeps the tree in blood, unearthing that inept memory,
oozing out, soiling the eyes of the vicuna…
I blot it out with desert hues, with torches, with dead
children, swept beneath the turbaned laughter.

Up there, on high, sleeps the father, up there where the star
awaits me, enthralled by my smile:
masques and starry, enshrouded corpses
wrenching each and every twisted nail from this body.

That tomb opens upon our every terror, intertwining
with the disasters of yesteryear, engraved behind my eye;
I survey the factious storm, I rein you in!

I travel along the scales, the very quivering length
of this serpent. And I nestle within the insect, and listen
to the pondering droves.

VIEUX CHIEN SE SOUVENANT

Il n'y a plus ici ni parole ni musique,
on n'y voit plus deux êtres se parlant pour se parler.
Ici la matière se soulève et casse l'homme.

Le silence rabote tes nerfs, te marque
du sceau cruel des scies hurlantes ;
les chaînes atrocement compriment tes chairs

comme à midi les tambours du tonnerre.

AN OLD LOWLIFE, REMINISCING

There is no trace left; no speech, no music;
no trace of these two beings talking to one another, just to talk.
Here, the evaporation of matter is enough to break a man.

The silence shaves your nerves, engraves you
with the harrowing signature of its howling saws;
atrociously, the chains constrain your flesh,

like the thunderous drums at noon.

ET LORSQU'ILS SE TAIRONT
à Léopold Sédar Senghor

Et lorsqu'ils se tairont, je dirais : "Va-t-en, vieux diable
mais non ! oh non ! reviens embellir l'épi fort
et le chant ridicule noué sur nos dos en hécatombes..."

Avec une musique que les cordes aigrissent,
ils nous emboîtent et nous ceinturent ;
avec leurs larmes où tu deviens têtard...

haches et mots durs ! Machettes
rouillant au râtelier primaire...
Mais qu'est-ce leur rabiot ? Dis-moi qu'est-ce ?

Nous même errant lambeau du seul
éclat qui fit de vous cette histoire, cet univers,
nous même avec nos raisons à mes trousses...

Serrant la virgule de très près et le nuage,
scindant ce sol, remuant le songe aveugle
et boitant, tout doucement boitant sur mon visage !

Où se tient donc ce Sud atroce
courant en éclairs sur vos langues et vos rétines ?
Ah ! dites où se tient le Sud précaire !

Dans vos genoux peut-être ? Prothèse énorme
du poète giclant vers l'être fui,
du poète mort sans prothèse !...

Et chaque fois que l'homme, mon Dieu, chaque fois
que l'homme
effleure la lumière, il lui tombe des pommes
ou des grenades dans le cœur...

AND WHENEVER THE SILENCE TAKES THEM OVER
for Léopold Sédar Senghor

And whenever the silence takes them over, I'll say: "Get lost, you old devil!
Wait, no! No, no! Come back, come adorn the great spike
and the absurdity of song knotting up our devastated backsides…"

With a music whose onset curdles the strings,
the strings surrounding us, restraining us
with tears, with tears that transform you into a pollywog…

Axes and cruel words! Machetes
gone to rust on the rack…
But what do they get out of all this? Tell me, what?

We, the endlessly wandering remnants of the sole
blast whose history made you, along with this universe,
We, with consciousness forever at our heels…

Clutching the comma of closeness alongside the cloud,
wrenching open the ground and rousing this dream, directionless,
limping, slowly and gently, across the contours of my face!

Where has this atrocious South led us,
coursing like lightning across your tongues and your eyes?
Ah! Tell me, where has this utterly unseemly South led us to!

Into your knees, perhaps? The enormous prosthesis
of the poet spewing the fleetingness of life,
the dead, prosthesis-less poet!…

And each and every time that man, my God, each and every time
that man
touches upon some light, it goes plummeting into his heart,
like apples or pome-grenades …

Mon Dieu, chaque fois que l'homme essaye d'être soi seul,
de lui-même surgissent des serpents antécédents,
des terres oubliées et des confidences âcres !

Homme ni vu ni connu, tarsier ruant,
s'enturbannant de nuits fastes et très sanglantes ;
ni la mer ni le ciel ni l'épouvantable rire ;

ni le sanglot ni l'or ni la neige ni mon doigt
portant le cuivre des nuits rebelles
sur une terrasse berbère ;

et ni l'océan que brise mon geste,
ni ton corps simplement étourdi par mon sourire,
assis, grignotant des criquets et des délires...

Homme poreux que la mémoire recèle,
...Tu-le, Seigneur, car il me faut poursuivre mon chemin...,
homme exaltant l'herbe, le ciel et les couleurs...

My God, each and every time that man tries to be alone with himself,
from that self springs the serpents of yesteryear,
the serpents of forgotten lands and pungent mystique!

Mankind: unseen, unknown, a tarsier let loose, run wild,
wrapped in turbans of dazzling and blood-soaked nights;
no sea, no sky, no awful laughter;

no sob, no gold, no snow, nor finger of mine
wearing the copper of rebellious nights
over an Amazigh terrace,

nor ocean breaks my stride,
and not even your body, whose motions come to a still before my smile,
settling in, grazing the crickets and the deliriousness…

Porous mankind, whose harbor is memory:
"…Sir, just kill him already, I've got to get back on my way…"
Mankind: exalting the grass, the sky, and all its many colors…

PERMANENCE DE TAOS AMROUCHE

Je vois Tipasa, l'inoubliable pilier millénaire,
je vois l'ombre du blé sur la mer ;
et les femmes comme les hommes numides de pleine
errance, je vois
l'aiguille des pics et la honte séculaire !
ils se déchirent sur le champ, ils me déchirent !
C'est l'amour qui exacerbe l'épouvantable buisson,
le torrent des Aurès ; c'est Kahina, dit-on,
qui procède au compte des vieux surgissements !

Peut-être rien, après tout, que la meule et la belle orge
et le berbère et le claquement de balles
et les timbales et les fêtes intermittentes
et la mort, enfin, bondie et qui recueille
en nous l'élixir agressif de l'atome.

D'avoir tourné le temps à ta faveur et tenu
jusqu'au bout — où l'on voit se convulser les Temps —
avec pour seule compagne une musique errante,
Mère, c'est en nous que ton soleil rayonne !
Il dresse sur nos rides, sur le pays un sang
neuf et si fort que se délitent les mémoires
de gel, Taos ! C'est encore là
que ton ombre plasmatique, entre veilles et rêves,
(incandescente de henné, ombre de calme reflet
gisant sur ma musique !) Ah ! c'est encore plus bas

où l'on fourbit les armes rouillées des mercenaires ;
où l'on dresse la tribu contre son sang !
où l'on fournit ses enfants au fournil !
où l'on pose ses pas sur la fourche du démon !...
Ah ! c'est encore plus bas, plus lointainement bas
que se tient, fripé, le grand sourire crispé

THE PERMANENCE OF TAOS AMROUCHE

I see Tipasa, the unforgettable thousand-year-old pillar,
I see the shadow of the wheat upon the sea;
and the Numidean women, like the men, of outright
aimlessness, I see
the sharp peaks and the age-old shame!
Tearing one another apart throughout the countryside, tearing me apart!
That's what love is, that which pushes the frightful bush to its limits,
the torrent of Aurès; that is Kahina, they say,
who continues to carry out the uprisings of old!

Perhaps nothing, after all, save the grindstone, and the beautiful barley,
and the Imazighen, and the resounding echo of bullets,
and the timpani, and the intermittent festivals,
and death, lastly, springing back to extract
the atom's assailing elixir from inside us.

Having turned the weather in your favor, having held on
to the very end—where the convulsions of Time can be surveyed!
With only a few stray notes of music as one's companion,
O Mother, the rays of your sun are breaking through us!
It hoists, above our shriveled skin, over the country, a blood
so new and so strong, Taos, that the frost-covered memories
begin to flake away! And there it is,
still, your plasmatic shadow, between waking and dreaming
(an incandescent henna, a shadow of calm reflection,
lying motionless over my music!) Ah!, but lower, still,

where the rusted weapons of mercenaries are brandished;
where the tribe is raised to oppose its own blood
where children are shoveled into ovens!
where footsteps travel along the demon's fork!...
Ah! But it's only further down below, even further down
one catches a glimpse of the aborted, contorted smile

des peuples atroces qu'on enjambe comme une tombe !

Debout parmi nous et dans ma nuit ionique !
aussi frêle, aussi belle dans ton manteau de roses,
debout dans ma voix, chroniquement debout,
avec moi sur les rires et les sanglots des nuits !

Fille de Nubie, fille des monts, ciel utérin !
nous-mêmes répudiés de nous-mêmes par le Commerce
geôliers de nous-mêmes et nous exilant très loin ;
fille du sable fin que décrivent les scinques !

Mais une belle jamais ne meure, mais une belle
jamais n'enfante autre chose que l'écrit vaste !
Une terre réprimée et qui revomit l'orge
sous le ciel ancien brûleur de vieux bâtons !
mais une belle voix cinglant l'espace aveugle
essore les nuées et libère nos coeurs acerbes !

Car parmi moi, debout sur la dune, sur le délire,
te voilà soufflant en vent si puissant et si doux
que les planètes exsudent nos morts et frémissent
de honte très lourde murée dans le silence !

Alors que ton éclat nuit aux étoiles précaires !

of one atrocious people, stepped over like a grave!

Looming around us, throughout my ionic night!
As lovely and soft, throughout, as your cloak of roses,
looming throughout my voice, chronically looming
me into the laughter, into the gentle sobs of evening!

Lady of Nubia, lady of the mountains, O uterine sky!
We repudiate ourselves by ourselves, by what we call Commerce;
we, ourselves, our own imprisoners, ourselves becoming the outcasts;
O lady of the skink-inscribed, delicate sands of the desert!

And yet a beauteous thing never dies, and yet a beauteous thing
bears no offspring other than the vastness of the written word!
A land forever repressed, a land forever spitting up barley
beneath the heavens, the ancient igniter of dried-out brush!
Yet still a beautiful voice, blistering the aimlessness of space,
arrives to wring out the clouds, and free our embittered hearts!

Because around me, over every dune, over every deliriousness,
is you, softly blowing in the wind, so powerful and so gentle
that the planets are forced to discharge our dead and tremble
with shame, weighing down upon and walling them up in silence!

Though to unhinged stars your nightly glow may seem unseemly!

TOMBEAU DE LÉON-GONTRAN DAMAS

Au moment vrai tout meurt, tout redevient puissant :
Dieu rattrape les peurs et les sangs dans ses songes
de neutrons... et reprend ce que le sable intente
aux éclats de nuits fastes, aux terreurs qui me dévastent.

Assis là, parmi vous, mages d'un temps d'étoile,
sur le dos des cicindèles en butte à vos crachats,
Damas ! Vieil or ! oh ! l'or épouvantablement
ramené grain à grain au cri pur des prophètes !

Chaque nuit t'est comptée en ce monde de mort lente
où tout corps se démembre et tout doigt renie sa main ;
et le jour même, le jour enchâssé dans tes nerfs
tourbillonne autour de toi en ferments inhumains.

Tu promènes ton âme d'hyperbole en chaos,
tu es l'enfant sans luminaire !
Taillé dans la poutre excellente des enfers,
tu suintes d'un vaste sommeil qui nous roidit.
— Autant qu'une chatière, les noms portés
se dissolvent avec l'infini des mémoires...
mais les corps errants, tués, les corps absents ?

Et nous-mêmes, pardi ! nous-mêmes,
équarrisseurs de terres, preneurs de ciels puants ?
Car les murs se souviennent, car ma tête répand

cet involucre en astre écrasé dans nos cœurs.
Je m'exhale des peurs et des fleurs, debout et mort,
schiste amer d'où mon œil retire, au lieu d'amours

voulues, l'aiguille qu'imprime aux roches un vieux délire !
Mais nous-mêmes debout, prisonniers de villes tueuses ?

THE TOMB OF LÉON-GONTRAN DAMAS

At the very moment everything dies, everything becomes powerful once again:
God catches a glimpse of the fear, the blood dwelling inside his
neutron dreams…, and seizes upon what the sands present
to the lightning-filled luxury of night, to the terrors that tear me apart.

Seated there, beside you, on the backs of the cicendelas, are mages
from an age of astral immersion, on the receiving ends of your phlegm,
Damas! The golds of old! Oh! The eeriness of the gold,
restored, bit-by-bit, to the puritanical screams of prophets!

Every night comes alive with you, in this world's slow death,
where every limb is lost, every finger drawn from its hand,
and even the dawn, enshrined in your every nerve, the dawn
whirls around you in a variety of inhuman fermentations.

You propel your hyperbolic soul into chaos,
you, the lamp-less child!
Carved from the exquisite beam of hellscapes,
you ooze from the vastest of dreams that congeal us.
—into a ventilation shaft, the names borne through
and dissolving into the infinity of memory…,
but what about the aimless bodies, killed in cold blood, the absent bodies?

And what about us, for that matter!, what about us,
executioners of earth, plunderers of putrescent heavens?
After all, the walls remember; after all, my head spews

forth this astral whorl that's squashed inside our hearts.
I breathe out fears and flowers; I, dead, but looming still,
a bitter schist through which my eye pulls, rather than unrequited

loves, the needle threading the old delirium through the rocks!
And what about us, still looming, prisoners of blood-thirsty cities?

Et de l'Ordre ! Ah ! brise cet ordre, enfant !

Errant parmi vos âmes ainsi qu'un fleuve en crue,
Damas depuis longtemps et depuis toujours présent
dans nos yeux, dans nos murs...

Je vais à toi plein d'orge nonpareille.
Et mort
de la mort du polyptère qui n'est autre que mon chant.

Et nous tous, jouxtant les haines
quand l'Afrique redresse ses cils,
bousculant les assassins...

Si dans nos corps la rue éclate de rire,
lus ensemble sur le pavé
en nerfs contus, en sangs

que relance et reprend telle une balle un chien !...

And the Order! Ah! Obliterate this order, child!

Wandering your souls like a river on the rise,
Damas, forever having been, forever you are; by our side,
inside our eyes, inside our walls…

I approach you, flush with unparalleled barley.
With death,
that deathly sort known to the dragonfish, which is my song.

And all of us, together, crossing streams of hatred,
as Africa curls her eyelashes,
queuing assassins…

What if, from deep within our bodies, the street were to break out
in laughter, spreading across the pavement in
mutilated nerves, in blood

roused and ready to take it all back, like a dog its ball!…

À XAVIER GRALL

C'est cette goutte de larme qui torture la mer,
ô sommeil qui promènes mon ombre ! C'est ce sol

inexplosé qui marche en moi, bouche tordue,
avec des caries des morts des meurtres des rires !

Pas à pas, je me souviens, j'oublie déjà ce corps
quand la mère était nue sous le pied du vieux hère !

Traînant ici ma bave, vieil escargot précaire,
quéquette au poing, j'allais déterrer le cimetière

où n'était qu'un palais écrasant nos colères !
Mais amandier ! putain d'amandier, tu riais !

Je marche quand se repose cet oiseau coprophage...
sans retour, sans futur, inondé par tes yeux !

Je leur ai tendu l'œil, les doigts croulant de mites ;
ma belle étoile, assez ! Je ne vois que ce Sud

sans mesure, sans exemple, jouant d'un grand sourire !
Je leur ai rendu le ciel tapissé de mes délires !

Shalom ! Salut ! Ahlan ! L'alfa cousait la terre,
mais il avait le pied qui pesait sur la mère !

La ciguë m'emboîtait le sang, la renoncule
et tous les chats présents feuilletaient l'univers :

homme, tu ne sais pas que je viens pour te déplaire !

Nous avons embelli l'azur de cette terre

FOR XAVIER GRALL

One teardrop: what tortures so terribly the sea, O dream;
you who make your way by way of my shadow!, this bed of soil,

undisturbed, making its way from within me, my smile twisted up
with the decay of the dead, the murderers, the maniacal laughter!

Step by step, I recollect; up to this point, I'd forgotten that body,
that moment: that mother, laid bare under the old wretch's boot!

Precarious old snail that I am, leaving a trail of slime as I go,
I equip my prick in hand, I exhume this palace, whose sole

purpose in this cemetery seems wiping out collective wrath!
But almond tree! O whorish almond tree, how you go on,

how you laugh! The coprophagous bird signals me: move along…
no looking back, no looking forward; your eyes, they take me in!

To them I offered one of my own, moth-eaten fingers in full view;
enough already, O beautiful star, enough! I see only a South

without bounds, without parallel, putting on its grandiose grin!
To them I offered a sky, sewn from my own delusions!

Shalom! Salut! Ahlan! The alfalfa was what wove this land together,
but it was the weight of his foot, the weight of his foot my mother felt!

It was hemlock which nested me in the blood, the ranunculus,
the stray cats slinking their way through the cosmos:

O mankind, do you not realize, I've come to strike a nerve!

We have embellished the azure of this land

avec des luminaires, pierres de lapidation

aux diables ! Homme sordide, voilà
l'enfant qui meurt, ballonné par tes agapes !

Debout... Je suis debout sur le delta d'un Nil
et j'écoute l'ahuri grain de sable et je grignote

ton nez royal, ô femme, et je chevauche l'éclair
sans miroir, sans mémoire, assis sur un tonnerre !

J'arrache la toile, ma peau, le corps n'est plus
qu'un soleil abominable, qu'un plasma inexplicable !

Ecrit tel une ride, aboli, très mal écrit
sur nos peaux, Seigneur mortel et mort, écrit

sur le vent que j'enténèbre, sur le blé que je suscite
autour de moi, honni par le rêve et le sommeil !

Je ne puis effacer comme un tableau chantant
ce sol où grince un socle, ni tes joues, ni ce timbre,

de lui s'élèvera l'aile et si mon silence
aux nuits dicte la mort, ta voix seule incendiera

nos fantômes épars, nos tribus qui d'escarres
nulles refont jaillir parmi moi la montagne !

O peuple que j'étrangle ! O vieux peuple entassé
et que ne trouve plus le chien chercheur de truffes !

Vois si je suis assis parmi toi, mais va-t-en !

with the light we shed, the stones we cast

at demons! Mankind, miserable mankind, thus
this dying child, bloated by your banquets!

Head raised…Here I stand, over the delta of the Nile–
I can hear the bewildered grains of sand, and I eat away

at your majestic nose, O woman, and I straddle the lightning,
the mirror-less, memory-less lightning; saddling the thunder,

I tear away this web I call my skin, the body turned a mass
of pure solarity, a mass of abominable, inexplicable plasma!

Written into the wrinkles, suppressed, atrociously written
into the surface of our skins: Lord deathly, deadly, dead; written

into the wind I wrap in shadow, into the wheat to which I give rise,
into the wheat that surrounds my body, scorned by dreams, by sleep!

That which I cannot erase; like a painting, a painting that intones
this soil, and into which neither your cheeks, nor this timber, grind,

but a plinth, a plinth whose wings take flight; and if my silence
spells a death out into the night, your voice alone will emblazon

the dissemination of our ghosts, our tribes, outfitted in
keloidal scars, and force the mountains up around me again!

O people, people that I strangle! O ancient people piled upon
people, who have lost track of the dog they sent to track the truffles' scent.

Look to see if I am down amongst you, but get out while you can!

DISPARITION DE LA NOVA

à Olivier Mongin

Elle a su retentir
et son ancien rire bourdonnant à mes oreilles,
mêlé aux ombres ruantes de la nuit,
fore mon sang et le retourne ; les pelleteuses
et les mémoires étranglent ce désert...

S'en aller, partir encore, criquet vert sans membrures,
avant d'éclater ici sous les décombres
et les rires et les fuites !...
Oh ! Sud assis en moi, je viens
debout dans la sourdine itinérante.

Exil, très simple exil exhaussé par mes crampes,
scintillant d'éclairs mûrs, excitant toute lune
en ces relents de tabac noir et m'éloignant
de l'arc-en-ciel précaire ! Exil !
mes pas seront les deltas, le pas des mers !

Car je suis le joueur qui tue la nuit sans carte,
le funambule tendu en corde tressée
à mesure qu'il avance sur le feuillet du temps,

le mur en haillons où tu écris ma vie,
vieux ciel plombé, tombé sous les caresses absentes.

J'ouvre pourtant mon cœur et j'y trouve un

vieux livre

phosphorescent.

O nuit marine !

THE NOVA'S DISAPPEARANCE

for Olivier Mongin

Well-versed in ringing out its song,
alongside its laughter, its antiquations, singing through my ears,
intermingling with the nightly shadows, ill-at-ease,
it drills my blood and reverses its course; the arms of excavators
and memories are strangling this desert...

Get lost, go, don't look back, O green and formless locust,
before you explode, here and now, beneath the debris,
the rolling laughter, the refugees!...
Oh! South deeply-enthroned inside me, see how I come,
how I rise to my feet, amidst nomadic muteness.

Exile: no more, no less; rising through my skin, spasming,
scintillating with overripened lightning, moving every moon
within these feints of black tobacco to ecstasy, drawing me
further from tenuous rainbows! Exile!
May my steps be the deltas and the footprints of the seas!

For I am the gambler, casting his lot to the card-less night,
the tightrope-walker, tense as braided rope,
making his way over the atmosphere's smoothed-out sheet,

the ragtag wall over whose length you scribble out my life,
those leaden heavens, felled beneath forever absent caresses.

Nevertheless, I open up my heart and remove an

old tome

of phosphorescence.

O seafaring night!

Déporté dans ces ruines, je m'arrête, brisé net...
Ficelles qui remplissent ma tête de chemins !
Je t'attends, gazelle, je t'attends !

Et j'annule,

j'annule les fourmis légionnaires, j'annule
le vent. Homme
hormis le soleil et trop d'ombre farcie d'yeux
je vais, irai si loin encore.
O femme, autour de moi, te délectant d'étoiles
lisibles dans ma nuit.

Deported to these ruins, I have come full-stop, utterly broken…
The ins-and-outs fill my head with aimlessness!
O gazelle, I lie in wait, I lie in wait!

                                    And I sound the end,

I sound the end to every last legionary ant, I sound the end
to the wind. One man,
foregoing the sun and the surplus of the shadows, clogged with eyes,
I continue, and I will continue on, to the beyond.
O woman, wrapped around me, taking your delight in what stars
might be made from a darkness like mine.

À LUCIEN BITTERLIN

Laissez-la vivre enfin !.. et qu'elle coure
vers les lionnes aux sauts parfaits...

Ecornée et ruant alentour, reprenant
le fil de l'eau jusqu'à la mare

tuée par sa psychée.

J'attends sans très bien savoir,
J'attends...

Mais ici tout est figé !
Mais ici tout est trop calme !

Ici le printemps perd ses rémiges...
— Et les visages, dis ! et les visages ?

FOR LUCIEN BITTERLIN

Let her live, at last!…so that she might rush
into the lion's den, in graceful leaps and bounds…

Dehorned, run amok, tracing
the stream of water back to the larger body

laid waste by her psyche.

I lie in wait, without really understanding why;
still, I lie in wait…

But now everything is frozen in place!
But now everything has grown too quiet!

Now, springtime has lost its pinions…
—And the faces, say something! And what about the faces?

SUR LA TOMBE D'EROS

Ce n'est que la route verte au comble
du soleil distendu et de la nuit brutale ;
l'escarpement qui du plus clair du lac
remonte vers mes yeux l'oripeau noir du ciel.

Elle vibre en cotylédon
et bruit de dunes que le vent
d'arcs insinue
en cette terre exfoliée.

Tourterelle de Chine, oiseau fou et sans rameau,
sais-tu que l'olivier foudroyé me tend entier
sur le miroir repris grain à grain ?

BEFORE THE TOMB OF EROS

Nothing less than the green road to the sun's
distended apogee alongside that of the brutal, brutal night;
the ridge that from the clearest of lakes,
makes its way back up the black rags of the sky, and into my eyes.

Resonating inside the cotyledon,
and the dunes' noisy dust, worming
windy insinuations
of an exfoliated earth.

Turtledove of the Orient, O mad and branch-less bird,
do you see how the lightning-struck olive tree draws my entirety
into the mirror, to be regained, grain by grain?

NUIT LIMINAIRE

Nuit belle hantée par le frémissement
du soleil sur la peau de l'éclatante berbère...
je grésille, volcan de mer,
sur ton corps blond et sur tes seins.

Voyageuse aux yeux violets,
je casse le pot et son démon.

Mais en sourdine, ô nuit d'appel et de rappel,
un corps triste, un corps très beau, au loin,
dans la grisaille agite mes nerfs et les distend
sur le pavé noir de mon sang.

Un corps très beau oublieux de mon corps,
un corps très simple.

THE LIMINARY NIGHT

What a beautiful night, haunted by the quivering
of sun over dazzling Amazigh skin...
a volcanic seascape, I sizzle
down the blondness of your body, your breasts.

A wanderer, with violet eyes,
I break open that which contains the demon.

But from the silence, O night of calling out and back again,
emerges a body of sadness, an extraordinarily beautiful body, somewhere
deep down in the gloom, stirring my nerves, expanding them
across the black pavement of my blood.

An extraordinarily beautiful body, oblivious to my own body,
a body, and nothing more.

CONFINS

Errant si seul parmi ton ciel, ô tourterelle,
vers la rampe d'éclairs bruités sur les flots
magiques d'enfances martyres

(Ici les lampes abritent la Lune !
la lame, bel oiseau, qui tranche ta carotide.
Mais à qui parler, qui
donc exhumer de la nuit d'où s'égoutte
le silence violent ?) ;

je jette le rêve aux sables mouvants
de ta lymphe, je jette au vent
ta glu et me voici
dissonant, m'élevant des miroirs et des musiques...

C'est l'éclat meurtrier
des quasars et du matin
loin du cloaque, hors ce malheur
que l'artisan dévide sans pleurer son cœur brûlé.

CONFINES

Wandering, so alone throughout your heavens, O turtledove,
toward the beacon of lightning, bristling over the mystical
waves of martyred childhoods

(Out here, lights undergoing negotiations with the Moon!
That blade, O beautiful bird, that drags itself across your jugular.
But who to talk to, who
to exhume from a night dripping with
violent silence?);

I dispose of the dream in the quicksand
of your lymph, hurling your birdlime
into the wind, wherein I become
the dissonance I am, rising from the mirrors, the music…

So goes the murderous glow
of quasars, of dawn,
far beyond any cloaca, beyond any of the ill-deeds
rolled out by its creator, letting no tears fall for his burnt-up heart.

CONTRE-JOUR

A l'océan toujours ce qui efface la nuit
d'un sésame à fleur des os :
galet d'étoile, rapt de chevaux.

Voyageur agité des strideurs du sang gommé,
pose ton corps écartelé sur l'or,
oublie le sol, oublie le ciel et vois

à contre-jour l'oryx asséchant le soleil.
Chaque matin s'éclaire de pies
t'empalant au nopal éclaboussé d'orages.

O clartés meurtrières, je suis assis, j'entends
l'hélianthe courbé
geindre dans les rémiges des oiseaux nécrophages.

AGAINST THE LIGHT

Throughout the ocean forever erasing the night
around a sesame flower's blooming bones:
starry pebble, equine abduction.

O wanderer, still writhing from the discord of backed-up blood,
unfurl your utterly run-ragged body across the gold,
forget about the earth, forget about the heavens, and look how

the oryx, its outline against the light, dries itself in the sun;
Each morning brings magpies to light,
impaling you upon the soaking wet, storm-drenched nopal.

O murderous clarity, here I am, sitting, listening
to the warped sunflower,
wailing from within the quills of necrophagous birds.

DÉSERT

Chien sauvage, très irascible, veux-tu
de mon ombre exprimer le désert douloureux ?

Chacal des nuits sans lune, viens danser sur la plaie
faste des jouis furieux.

Je vous donne des heures contuses qui suppurent
par le bec du corbeau.

Toute une ville hantée de fous déterre
des chemins en lambeaux.

Mes atomes cliquettent en étoiles filantes
dans les larmes retenues.

Hyènes errantes, brisez ce corps sur le poli
des nues.

DESERT

Irascible and wild dog, would you like
my shadow to express the misery of this desert?

Jackal of moonless nights, come dance upon the splendorous
wound of furious dawns.

I offer you the contused hours of days festering
from the crow's beak.

An entire city, haunted by madmen, unearthing
the gone-to-hell streets.

My atoms whirling together into shooting stars
behind the held-back tears.

Errant hyenas, tear this body apart over the clouds'
gloss.

À KELTHOUM

Sur les chemins d'exil et d'étoiles, tu marches
jouant avec le sable, avec la nuit et l'eau
consumée par tes paupières...

N'était la roue, je serais le marbre amer
se brûlant à tes yeux... aux mémoires
sans timbre et sans pagaie.

Je brûlerai mon or au couchant de cambouis ;
mais je reviens vers toi dans la sourdine
des phytosonges portant à ma ceinture
l'impeccable année-martyre.

FOR OUM KALTHOUM

Out along the exile-paved streets and stars, you go,
playing with the sand, the night and water
consumed by your eyelids…

If it weren't for the wheel, I would be the bitter marble
ablaze with your eyes…, with your memories;
no oar in sight, no sound.

I will set my gold on fire in the setting of the sun's oily sludge;
however, I promise to come back for you, through the muted
phyto-reveries, and from my side I will be carrying
this impeccable martyr of a year.

CERCLE

Ici tout cercle tourne autour du Cercle ;
les rayons, les gluons empierrés, les torsions,
le pavé, le grès du pressoir... Ici la roue
épouvantable du jour
inconnu me tord le cou.

Le cercle se ferme dans tes yeux de chorales
et de pleureuses
assises, stipe offert au silence, au vent
du jet de sang criant
les noms inertes...

Je te vois couchée. Au loin,
les pluviers répètent l'écumeuse
violence
du sable ;
couchée sur la dalle au salon dur sans boussole.

Les terreurs tanguent à mes yeux, mes cheveux
d'où tu reviens te roulant
me déroulant, grand migrateur,
sur un clavier d'étoiles sans contemplation.

CIRCLE

Every circle here takes its turn around the great Circle;
the cosmic rays, the gravelly surface of gluons, the twists and turns,
the city streets, the wine-presses…Here the fearful
wheel of the unknown
dawn twists its way around my neck.

The circle seeks closure in your eyes, like a choir
or women in the downward spirals
of mourning, a flower stem given over to silence, to wind,
on behalf of bloodstreams screaming out
motionless names…

I watch you lying there. In the distance,
the plovers trail the spumy
violence
of the sands;
lying on the flagstone in the tense, directionless salon.

The terrors pitch and keel their way through my eyes, my hair,
from whence you return, unraveling yourself,
which in turn finds me unraveling, in my great migration,
over a claviature of stars, unconsciously.

FÊTE

Demain, ils changeront leur ville en abattoir ;
ils se soûleront du sang de la bête, du fumet
des braises et de remugle. Demain,

les yeux, tous les yeux s'assiéront sur le billot
brûlant
des trépidations, des cris, des larmes.

Mais rien ! Rien
ne miroitera.

Termitières, fondrières, égouts, gadoues
Sodomes, enfants
oubliés sur le trottoir, dansez
dans la ténèbre !

CELEBRATION

Tomorrow, they will transform their city into a slaughterhouse;
they will drink themselves drunk on the blood of the beast, the aroma
of embers and wretched stenches. Tomorrow,

the eyes, the eyes of everyone will settle upon the chopping block
aflame
with fear, with screams, and with tears.

But nothing! Nothing
will sparkle.

Termite mounds, potholes, sewers, marshes,
Sodoms, children
orphaned to the streets: dance,
dance in darkness!

PERDITION

à Brahim Lehiany

Fauconnier solitaire brandissant ton cœur nu
pour gaver ton oiseau disparu dans la prunelle
ardente des soirs d'orages fauves ;

Fauconnier, sans raison, sans musique, tu vas,
tu viens tournant en rond et sans relâche
sur la rocaille où sèche le rêve ;

tu grandis, tu t'amenuises, sifflé
par le haje irrédentiste, le geai rieur...
par ton arme perdue, digérée par le ciel ;

Fauconnier fou, l'amour est un brandon,
un tison que le silence
apaise.

PERDITION

for Brahim Lehiany

Lone falconer, brandishing your forced-open heart
to force-feed your bird: that which merely disappears into the fiery
gaze of the stormy, swarthy nights;

O falconer, off you go, devoid of reason, devoid of music,
and back you come again, whirling round and round, unceasingly
over the scree where dreams run dry;

you grow, you dwindle, subjected
to the hissing of the naja haje, the laughing jay...,
to your lost arm, swallowed by heavenly intestines;

Mad, mad falconer, love is a firebrand,
a branding-iron quenched
by silence.

MIGRATION

Aloès perdu dans le sommeil des singes
et qui de l'arbre écoute la mort,
autour du feu sanglant, j'agis

avec les oiseaux de mer qui s'en iront
frémissants dans la lumière,
oubliant la poudrière.

Je te regarde, oiseau, bel oiseau qui volettes
de la steppe à la Lune
en hématines ; je dis

que la vague est un caillou. Bel oiseau, si tu vois
le désert, reprends-le !

MIGRATION

Aloes, lost somewhere in the dreams of the macaques,
in whosoever, from the treetops, hears death
circulate the bloody fire; I do

as the birds over the sea do, who fly away,
quivering at dawn,
oblivious to the powder keg.

I watch you, bird, O beautiful bird, as you dart
from the steppe to the Moon's
hematine; I say

a wave is a grain of sand. O beautiful bird, if you see
the desert, bring it back around!

NIGHT-CLUB

La mer suppurée de musiques se roule
et creuse si bien ton cœur
que tout s'assèche autour de toi :
maisons et murs, arbres et routes ;
hommes allant, cerceaux d'abois
aux coups denses de fusils...

Les femmes, encore debout, danseront, intrépides...
Que d'elles me vienne le vent
ajusteur du baobab,
Corsaire redressé sur l'éclat de la Terre !

Que d'elles ! connaissant toutes les racines
— les ravines et les rapines —
m'advienne
le vieil oiseau-fascine
en corps décrit, en sable empreint
du soleil sinistré !

Ville ordinaire, un cancrelat te vide,
grand chien sans tique !
automnal et malsain !
il te vide du songe des morts
quand la Lune virevolte, quand la semelle alarme
le pli noir des étoiles.

NIGHT CLUB

Festering with music, the sea rolls over
and delves so deeply into your heart
that everything around you evaporates:
the houses, the walls, the trees and roads;
the men on the go, the baying echoes
Of rifles, loading, unloading…

The women, regardless, go on dancing, dauntless…
That the women would grant me that same wind,
stylist of the baobab trees,
that Corsair looming over the Earthly glow!

That they would!, conscious of all the roots
—the ravines, the rapines—
usher the old
mesmerismic-bird my way
through a descript corpus, through sands imprinted
by the disaster-stricken sun!

Unextraordinary city, one single cockroach sucks you dry,
you great tick-less dog!
Autumnal and malnourished!
Just one—sucking you dry of every last dream of the dead,
as the Moon turns on its heels, treads disrupting
the darkened fold of the stars.

AN NEUF

Voyez leurs ailes fripées ; leur bec crochu
déterre en le grimoire l'inceste...
et l'insecte étoilé de cambouis et de sang

Voyez leurs serres, leur barbe qui balaie
de ma raison l'exsudation
des raisons et des mémoires !

Prophètes sans le sou entonnés par les peuples,
prophètes sans cité où le neurone avance
en éclairs fulgurants...

Le ventre de la nuit peuple de vastes ravages
ta tignasse cendrée, oiseau clair qui circules
dans les bolongs, dans les absences.

Les femmes assises dans le sous-sol répètent
la triste, cruelle chanson
des nourrissons précaires...

Je vois... je te vois frémissante dans le stipe
du vent, dans la poussière. Cailloux,
reprenez ce désert !

"Abran*", si tu reviens voler mon coq,
défonce la toile d'épeire ; déguste
le sale poisson ! "

— Je ne mange pas de ce pain là !...
L'insecte vrombit, efface l'ocelle,
l'espace corrige le sol coureur.

---

* Abran: chat sauvage en berbère.

NEW YEAR

See their crumpled wings, their hooked beaks
disentomb the grimoire, every incest...,
alongside every insect, shining out like a star amid the oil, the blood...

See their talons, their beard, sweeping aside
what reasons and recollection
my reason exudes!

The prophets, penniless, are intoned by an entire people,
prophets without a city, where neurons forge
themselves into flashes of lightning...

The belly of night, the people of widespread devastation,
your mane's glowing embers, luminescent bird weaving
every bolong tree, every absence.

The women underground keep repeating
the sad, cruel song
of precarious nurslings...

And I watch..., I watch as you shiver in the windy
stipe, in the dust. O grains of sand,
take back that desert!

"Abran˙, should you return to steal my rooster,
tear through the orb weaver's web; savor
its unsavory poison!"

—I want no part in this!...,
the insect thrummed, erase his ocellus,
this ground-dweller could use some space.

---

* Abran: wild cat in Tamazight

Je ne veux rien ! C'est dans la rue
que va fleurir l'épée ; le clou rouillé sanglote
à l'intérieur de toi ;

je ne veux rien, je suis ici,
tu vas, tu viens - la chaîne écoute
et l'arbre absout.

Si ce n'est qu'un tonnerre, une errance,
si ce n'est qu'un solfatare
épouvanté suant ses glaires !...

Un miracle accroché au néant des racines ;
je viens,
livré aux cornes

qui dessinent dans ma nuit l'astéroïde, l'oryx
et l'ambre ;
chevalier tueur, crieur, écoute

le vieux nègre désolé
adjurer le papayer
de lui donner l'œil trouble du crotale

I want nothing! It is in the streets
that the sword flowers; the rusted nail weeps
inside you;

I want nothing; here I am,
you come, and you go—the chain listens
and the tree absolves itself.

What if there is but one thunder, one aimlessness,
what if there is but one dreadful
Solfatara, just one that's willing to pour its phlegm forth!...,

But one miracle clinging to the nothingness of roots;
Here I come,
given over to the horns

tracing the asteroid through my night, through the oryx
and the amber;
O murderous, screaming knight, listen

to the sorry old negro,
how he implores the papaya tree
to let down the rattlesnake's cloudy eye.

DIASPORA

à Abdessamad Mouhieddine

La nuit collait à ma rétine, ne faisait qu'une
avec la pierre en cette mare d'étoiles...
Vieux diamant, l'œil et la danse suppriment
et aveuglent ma nuit au point du jour, au terme
de la vague sans musique, sans oiseau...

Océan, j'entends la diaspora guerrière
et la blancheur du coton noir ;
j'entends les chaînes qui s'entrechoquent...
Au fond des cales je vois le nègre
gratter ses rides, crier...
Je le sens qui me gratte.

Mon amour en allée dans la ténèbre !

Je vois l'enfant jaillie des sources :
Tiznit ! Sous le galet se dresse
à nouveau son nuage.
Oiseau, l'abeille n'est pas
au muret... le silence
du torrent pleut cruel.

Mon amour effeuillé fuyant ma fuite
avec les tiers premiers les tiers derniers
quand tout fourmille autour des crampes
d'échos et de veinules... Quand le fucus
éclate,
marcheur !

Mon amour, je flamboie, mortel et sûr,
tectonique et de neutrons ; je rabote
mon cercueil vêtu de peaux
et de tonnerres.

DIASPORA

for Abdessamad Mouhieddine

The night took a liking to my eye, becoming one
with this stone, floating its pool of stars…
Old diamond, the eye and its darting are enough of a suppression,
eclipsing my night into the early dawn, into the crest
of a wave: bird-less, music-less…

I can hear the warlike diaspora, O ocean, sounding outward,
and the white corollary of the black-sprouted cotton;
I can hear the links of the chain as they rattle, one against the other…
Down in the holds of the ship where I spy a negro,
screaming, clawing at his shriveled skin…
I feel him, too, clawing from within.

So my love descends the darkness!

And I see the child, sprung from the springs:
Tiznit! Its cloud
rearisen from the rock.
O bird, there's not a wasp to be found
beyond that wall…That cruel, continual
weeping to which you lend your ear is merely the river's.

O love, stripped of feathers, fleeing my flight
alongside the first of worlds, the last of worlds,
as everything begins to swarm the muscles,
spasming with echoes and venules…, as fucus
erupts,
O passerby!

My love, I am committing myself to flames: lethal and steadfast,
tectonic and neutronic; I am designing my coffin
the way I see fit, adorned with skin,
and sworn to thunder.

TOILES

Il faudra te nettoyer les oreilles des toiles
d'araignée qui s'y fabriquent ; mauvais tissage !

Il te faudra oser, toujours oser crever
l'œil trop calme du cyclone...

et construire en toi le miroir où l'on voit
courir en mer le cheval mort de l'éclipse,

sans que le courlis roulis d'ailes puissantes
que je porte au soleil mal compté ; sans soleil.

La barque, au crépuscule, taille le grégaire nuage
en étincelles, en escarbilles.

WEBS

What woven wickedness; let's clear the ears of that tulle,
what spider-webs are toiling away inside your skull!

Let's grow that spine of yours, a spine that will forever puncture
the serenity of the cyclone's eye, coming about...

to construct a mirror, from the interior, allowing you to watch
the dead horse of the eclipse run up and down the shoreline,

without the whirling, the curlews of passion-fueled wings
I wear, among the misleading rays of sunlight; without a sun.

At twilight, the ship proceeds to shave away the sheep-like haze
into scintillations, into cinders.

TEMPS NONPAREIL

C'est moi aussi quelque part dans un temps nonpareil
sans fleur, serti de vraies chitines ;
prisonnier de la terre morte, prisonnier
d'images, de sons terrant
le parler fort de la terre.

Quelque part, le marécage travaille, le sable
pense ; une lagune
érode le roc.

En mon sang se brise, debout,
l'accointance des roses inertes ;
le pays fourbit son arme, endosse
à nouveau son tonnerre.

Tout le pays écoute et rit,
tout le pays se gratte la chair,
sans sommeil et sans étoile.

A TIME UNLIKE ANY OTHER

I, too, am out there somewhere, in a time unlike any other,
flowerless, fixed in the unassailable chitin;
a prisoner of dead earth, a prisoner
of images, of sounds holing up
the whole mouth of earth.

Somewhere out there, the swamp labors, the sand
ponders; a lagoon
erodes the rock.

Out of my blood bursts the looming
acquaintance of dormant roses;
the country polishes its pistol, embracing
its old maelstrom once again.

The whole country pricks up its ears, laughs,
the whole country drags its claws across its flesh,
sleeplessly, starlessly.

TITRIT N'TD GGAT*

Quelques galets : le torrent
sur les brisants en bave lunaire,
oh ! latérites !

Et toi venue lavée de vents solaires,
venue du fond du cœur tracé de dolomites
si violemment que le miroir recouvre
en son eau l'impala.

Nous sommes huit autour de toi, Soleil,
debout sur tes flammèches.
Les vrilles rapides décomptent
en mon œil ton rhizome.

Cheval fou, galop simple, envolée de javelles
au vent rué de cliquetis...
Banc de sable rétréci, grain de sable que j'écoute,
l'automne est feuillet noir, c'est une larme
au bout des matins et des soirs.

Ichneumon, veux-tu voir le brasier et l'oiseau
que terre et ciel rudoient ?
Veux-tu gober le vent joueur de phéromones
à petit feu dans tes ocelles ?

Et s'éclairer en toi, coccyx aveugle
un hiver mauve te blanc
d'amandier ? Veux-tu voir
la forêt crucifiée ?

Te résigneras-tu à n'être qu'une cendre
sur le rocher si lisse, roulée, colombe

---

* La planète Vénus

116

TITRIT N'TD GGAT*

One, maybe two pebbles: the torrent's
lunar drool roused up, over the breakers,
Oh!, laterite!

And out you rush, washed over by solar winds,
out you rush from the depths of the heart, outlined in dolomite,
with such a violence that the mirror again sweeps
its waters over the impala.

There are eight of us encircling you, O Sun,
every flare-up underfoot.
The swiftness of the tendrils extract
your rhizome from my eye.

Mad horse, gallop so easy, a rush of javelins
through the wilding, noisy air...
O shrunken sandbank, O grain of sand to whom I listen,
autumn is a leafy black, a teardrop
that hangs from days and nights.

O ichneumon, how would you like to see inferno and bird
harassed by earth and sky alike?
How would you like to absorb the wind, that juggler of pheromones,
gently into your ocelli?

And illuminate from inside you, O visionless coccyx,
an almond tree's winter, mauve
and ghostly? How would you like to see
the forest, that crucified forest?

Will you resign yourself to nothing but ash,
upon a rock as smooth, as well-rounded as this one is, O dove,

---

* The planet Venus

autour du stipe grégaire,
houleuse de sternes et d'exocets ?

Circonscrit grain à grain, aigue-marine,
et muré dans ta cornée,
j'allume de lettrines
les doigts de fées absentes.

while around you circles the mindless fold of the frond,
swelling with seabirds and flying fish?

Confined bit by bit, colored aquamarine,
and enclosed inside your cornea,
I illuminate the faintest
touch of absent faeries with lettrines.

SIROCCO

Le soleil au sang ferreux trace à coup de scalpel
sur le cuir vert des nuits ton visage en détresse ;

d'ici gicle, tourbillonnaire, le souffle blanc
de la mort. D'ici s'élève,

ô nuit rayée du jour, le frémissement de la femme.

Extradé de la mémoire, réimprimant au songe
mes pas scindés d'ethnies de spectres ;

Suffète au bord des larmes, je déroule
ce ciel en vol d'outardes

sur la vague qui ferraille à la racine
de l'olivier couché en natte.

Mais c'est la nuit ! Et le grillon répète la guerre !
C'est la nuit du troglodyte lapidaire,

ceint d'éclats de granit ;
une nuit fixée aux boutres de Cafrerie

et qui du sol exsude le guet-apens.

SIROCCO

The iron of the sun's blood traces the distress of your face
onto the leathery green of sundown with the flick of a scalpel;

And out of that squirts the ghostly breath of death,
swirling through the air. And out of that arises,

O dawn-streaked night, the tremors of woman.

Extradited from memory, imprinted with illusion,
come my steps, splintered into spectral ethnicities;

O Shofet, on the verge of tears, I will roll this sky out
into a flurry of airborne houbaras, twirling

above the wave steeling itself against the twisted
braids of the olive tree's roots.

But night has fallen! And the cricket is rehearsing for war!
Tonight is the night of the lapidary troglodyte,

encircled by shards of granite;
a night paralyzed by the Kaffrarian dhows,

whose soils seethe the sensation of a sting.

ROUGE-GORGE

à Léopold Sédar Senghor

Miroitant rouge-gorge en ton éclat de corail
à contre-jour des socs rouilles,
cinglant de nacre et de cavales
l'équinoxe étiré...

en ton chant vers l'éclair où le Masaï ajuste
la jugulaire
(Sine si calme au filigrane de la Terre),
la lithobie m'innerve

d'orchidées crépusculaires.

Vigoureux autant que toi, frégate fendant
la mer,
qui déposes un trident
dans le bleu de mon cœur,

il incendie la forêt de bouleaux et crépite
sur le front du chasseur...
et de son bec écrit
mon sommeil mal rêvé.

REDBREAST

for Léopold Sédar Senghor

Shimmering redbreast, with your coral sheen
silhouetted by the rusted-out plowshares,
sailing from the mother-of-pearl and mares,
from this equinox, stretched out…

and into your song, heading for the lightning-outfitted
jugulars of the Maasai
(the Sine traveling the Earth's filigree so freely),
the lithobius shocks my nerves

with crepuscular orchids.

As vigorously as you, O frigate parting
the open seas,
burying a trident
in the blueness of my heart,

he sets fire to the birch-filled forest, sizzling
above the hunter's brow…
and from his beak pours the script
of my poorly-dreamt sleep.

CHANT DU SIGNE

(1)

Sur le fil des haines noueuses
d'estomacs, tu danseras
dégorgeant en caillots noir d'éclipses...

Enfant médaillé d'astres, paré de haches,
démembre-toi
comme le lion vieux de la mort !

Bois le ciel au goulot...
Au corps à corps, tue-le
en un sursaut de misérables rémiges.

(2)

Et à force de rire, le ciel pleure ses étoiles;
il les brise en enfants morflés, arqués
sur le trottoir...

le ciel épand sa bucolique
dans les galets et le sillon
mais j'éclaire la nuit triste

en diadème arquant l'enfant
cassé, soudé au sang
qui ennuage mon cœur.

SONG OF THE SYMBOLIC

(1)

You will dance the length of the string of viscerally-
knotted vitriol, spewing
sequentially into eclipse-black blood clots...

O child, decorated with stars, adorned with axes,
dismember yourself
like the age-old lion of death!

Drink in the sky...
Kill it, using only your hands,
one single upswing of feathery quills.

(2)

And by the dint of laughter, the sky weeps for its stars;
it shatters them into abused children, bowing
down on the sidewalk...

the sky spreads its bucolic
across the stones and furrows
but I illuminate the night's gloom

into a diadem stringing the bowed,
broken child, welded to the blood
that clouds my heart.

PRINCIPES DU PRINTEMPS

à Najib-Abdallah Refaïf

Il revînt, musette au flanc ; sa mule
interrogeait la mort serpente :
le chaos fouaillait à sa rétine
en chocs, en erres démentes.

Effeuilleur d'orages où niche l'amante !
demande au vent l'écrit brûlé,
le solstice et la détente
du colibri et de l'effraie !

Il te porte un éclair en anneaux de noctuelles,
un diadème d'aubes blanchies
aux fureurs des crépuscules,

faucheuse gammée d'estocs, d'amers
Cicones !

quand tu l'égouttes en lucioles
à la racine des menthes.

PRINCIPLES OF THE SPRINGTIME

for Najib-Abdallah Refaïf

He returned, satchel at his side; his mule
questioned the deathly writhe:
chaos whipped in distress
drifting with dementia through its eyes.

Defeatherer of tempestuous love-nests!,
beg the wind for a burnt script,
a solstice, and a respite
from the hummingbird and marsh owls!,

And it hands you the moth-loomed lightning,
a diadem of dawns whitened
in the twilight's fervor,

a reaper molded from rapiers, from bitter
Cicones!

as you proceed to strain its glow worms
through the mint root.

MAUVAIS SANG

C'est sur ce cœur mauvais
que j'écris avec mes yeux
et ma peau ruisselante
de rutilances enfilées dans le chas de l'aiguille.
O mon peuple assis sur la natte, il s'édite
un ordre qui te dévide ! Écoute
au fond de toi parler
le nécessaire nuage
et le fagot d'étoiles
où l'oubli tend sur l'ombilic le rire
du paysan qui de ses rides exhume la fleur
caressée de soleil ;
et la femme occultée,
malheureuse, mauvaise !...
agitant
les solennels tonnerres.

Je suis d'ici, debout sur le rocher très rouge
dans l'écrit des rétines,
du glucose éblouissant tes larmes,
tes alarmes et tes armes,
ta minuscule engeance
où se dressera Dieu
piqueté de clous verts.

Ah ! mon exil, intente à la cohue
cette lune d'acier
et délivre ce sol,
la glaise, le sang, le ciel
du cruel souvenir !
Orge, afin de savoir
la tablette et la toilette absurde
des danses de l'aloès.

FORLORN BLOOD

Over this forlorn heart
I pour out my eyes
and my streaming flesh
gleaming like strings through the eye of a needle.
O my people laid out over the mat, an order
has been decreed that will be your undoing! Just listen
to the quintessential cloud
and starry firebrand
scripted down, deep down inside you
where the peasant's laughter, having traversed the umbilicus
of oblivion, exhumes from his wrinkles, one sun-
caressed flower;
and one woman, obscured,
sorrowful, and miserable!…,
who stirs
the thunder's solemnity.

My home is a stone's throw from here,
in the retinal scripts of laterite,
from the enchanting glucose of every tear,
fear, and armory that steers
your insignificant spawn
where God rears his ungodly head,
speckled with green spikes.

Ah!, exile, bring this steeled moon
down into the crowded
pandemonium, and deliver this soil,
clay, blood, and sky
from the cruelty of memory!,
O Barley, so that we may bear witness
to the absurd tablet and toiletry
of dancing aloes.

OVERDOSE

à Abdallah Akchouch

Que ton sang mal écrit sur les murs de la mémoire
fuse en océan vert hennissant dans la myéline
en volée simple d'éclairs !
rouisseur qui du silence du séquoia démure
la boue
et le trèfle fugueur.

C'est la musique absente
de ce sol miséreux,
l'aigle au sanglot d'archet —
caillou fébrile et sûr —
entonné d'estocs, de dagues
par ton œil aux cils cabreurs...

Une terre où le sang démâte la goélette
jusqu'aux moutures
jusqu'aux boutures,
bondissante de zèbres, ruant d'okapis éclaireurs
dans ton corps agitateur :

océan frémissant dans la peau des terreurs
si furieusement
que s'exaltent les madrépores
dans le souffle crieur
de la trombe et des résines
de l'été et des sourdines.

Façonneur de temps rompus en cercles,
en orgies, en oiseaux
englués sur l'asphalte,
mortellement couchés,
pantelant sur le sabre

OVERDOSE

for Abdallah Akchouch

May your blood poorly scrawled across the walls of memory
run off into the oceanic greenery wailing inside the myelin
of lightning bolts!,
O retter, stripping the mud and fugitive
clover
from the sequoia's silence.

This is the music lost
on miserable soil,
the eagle in the woeful sob of the bow—
the feverish, steadfast stone—
intoned by the rapier, by the dagger,
by the upswing of your every last eyelash…

A land whose blood sucks the schooner's mast
down into the mulch,
down into the sediment,
surmounted by zebras, dredged up by the okapi
who scout your incendiary body:

A skin of terrors quivering over the oceans
with such fervor
that the madrepores are hoisted
by the howling breath
of summertime waterspouts
and resins and the silences that follow.

O fashioner of time, torn into circles,
into orgies, into a flight of birds,
bogged down by the asphalt,
nestled into its deadly glue,
panting their reflective agonies

reflétés d'agonies,

je te vois investi
par la douceur
très solidaire
du photon de lasers qui de ma lymphe écrit
l'aube sur le pisé
de l'errance ordinaire.

against a sword,

I see you vested
by the unified
sweetness
of laser photons using my lymph to spell out
the dawn across the adobe
of prosaic wandering.

MONTAGNE RIEUSE

Mastiqueuse, rieuse
en involucres de soldanelle...
Accoucheuse d'hirondelles,
d'ombelles et de ciguës,
n'obtempérant jamais
quand l'alcool bat tes nerfs
d'une sagaie flétrie
par moi, si juste, mal ajusté ;
éclaboussée de cigognes,
d'absinthes et de Cicones,
sans accroc et qu'un sable
inutile pétrit.
Mastiqueuse et tueuse, je suis
le soleil suicideur
en vertu de la nuit qui efface ton œil,
en vertu des majeurs
dromadaires sillonneurs.
Mastiqueuse, querelleuse absoute
par l'or,
fabuleuse et haïe,
je te vois
très gluante
sans rémission, avec
autour de moi
la mort
cachée dans ma poitrine
et dans ton cœur.

LAUGHING MOUNTAIN

O masticator, laughing
up through the involucres of soldanella...
Swaddler of swallows,
of umbels and hemlock,
forever intolerant
once the liquor hits your nerves
like an assegai, severely wilted,
by yours truly, so just, so maladjusted;
cyclones full of of storks,
of absinthe, of Cicones,
unimpeded and kneaded, uselessly
by the useless sands.
O masticator, O executioner, here I am,
the suicidal sun,
by virtue of the evening, into which your eye dissolves,
by virtue of the major
dromedary furrowers.
Masticator, O quarreler absolved
by gold,
mystical and loathed,
I see you,
absolutely viscous,
unforgivable, with
death
all around me,
locked away inside my chest,
inside your heart.

PSAUME 2005
(TOMBEAU D'ALIOUNE DIOP)

J'assèche mes larmes aveugles
au foyer de l'ellipse, sur la Saga
de la vie parolière...

Alioune
si formidable en ta tunique d'éther.

Tu imprimes la rose claire
à nos visages tectoniques
qui te découpent à froid, Grand Ciseleur !
sur le chemin des fourmilières.

Zinnia ! Zinnia ! je t'aimerai
d'impeccable brûlure
fendillée de mamelles
où minuit fixe ma larme.

Tu solennises la Lune courbée
d'étés
sursautant de porphyre,
de fuseaux et de foudres !

Car c'est d'Ur et de Dakar que ta vesce fleurie
de sisal et de fer
déploie, très calme, les dieux simples de la terre.
Alioune !

la cécité frappe l'homme goulu
au museau des reliques
du ciel brimé qui s'étiole
comme un trouvère grimé :

PSALM 2005
(THE TOMB OF ALIOUNE DIOP)

I hang my visionless tears to dry
in the foyer of an ellipsis, over the Saga
of lyrical life...

Alioune,
so formidable in your tunic of aether.

You impress the clearest of roses
into our tectonic glances,
those that cut into you so coldly, Great Chiseler!,
en route to the anthills, swarming.

Zinnia! Zinnia! I pledge my love
to you, with the impeccably
inflamed blaze of udders
that midnight fastens my tears to.

You solemnize the crescent Moon
of summers,
springing from the porphyry,
from the bobbin lace and lightning!

For it was out of Ur and Dakar that your vetch flowered
with sisal and iron,
deployed with tranquility, these unassuming gods of the earth.
Alioune!

Blindness strikes the glutted fool
with the muzzling relics of the sky,
a tormented sky, withering
like a gussied-up troubadour:

Nocturne ! Nocturne !
éraillée d'éclairs contus
grimaçant sur le couteau...
rassembleuse reptilienne
irradiant ma mémoire,
te taffetant de miroirs
utopies tendres
du sang
enlacé par mes nuits !

Alioune !
Terranga ! Terranga !
à ton âme houleuse.

Nocturne! Nocturne!,

rasping with contused lightning,

contorted along the length of the blade…

reptilian reassembler,

irradiating my memory,

inflecting you with the soft

utopian taffeta

of blood,

entwined with my night!

Alioune!

Terranga! Terranga!

to your soul, your turbulent soul.

RÉSURRECTION DES FLEURS SAUVAGES

Mon sang est cet étrange passant...
vaisseau bien cargué, voile déchirée
dans la nuit vétuste des vents.

Il ravage contus de soi seul, il savoure
ton sang, ô nuit
grise et bleue sous la cape
des criquets moites.

As-tu vu poindre le ciel fervent ?

Quand ses démons l'élancent, sans bannière, il massacre !...
Il tord le cou aux peuples secrets...

Et tire sur l'enfant magnifique du printemps.

On enchaîne l'ermite, on flagelle
l'enfant...

Je suis d'entre les hères et les laissés pour compte !

toute la terre s'ébranle, se fend,
tout le pays exhale
l'augure cruel.

Abadan ! Tabriz sans l'ombre
de son silence ! Tabriz martyre
en tes décomptes de honte !

Larme efflanquée, soleil où crève
la peau des mères
à l'aube des mitrailles, sur des nattes, sur des outils.

RESURRECTION OF WILDFLOWERS

My blood is this strangeness of a thing that drifts on by…
a well-rigged vessel, its sail torn to shreds
by the obsolete winds of the night.

Consuming its own wounds, it licks the blood
from your fingers, O blue
and gray night beneath the drapery
of dewy crickets.

Have you witnessed the fervor of the sky breaking?

Once its demons send the flagless thing flying, the massacre begins!…
It wrings the neck of its people kept under wraps…

And sets its sights on the magnificent child of springtime.

Chaining the hermit down, beating the child
senseless…

I am one with these wretches and outcasts!

The whole earth quakes, splits open,
the whole country exhales
its cruel omen.

Abadan! Tabriz without the shadow
of its silence! Tabriz, the martyr
of your shameful dealings!

Emaciated teardrop, sun beneath which
the skin of mothers is shriveling
in dawn's shrapnel, over the mats, over the tools.

Sur l'asphalte, sur le naphte épandu
en caillots sur les routes...
quand on porte ses morts

au cimetière,
nu, ordinaire...
tous marchent
piétinant le sol où furent
démembrés leurs ancêtres.

délivre mon corps de ce corps !

délivre-moi
des souvenirs !

Car je relève la tête et j'arme
un sang neuf, bien cargué, voile au vent.

Over the asphalt, over the naphtha dispersed
in clot after clot by the wayside...
when we haul its dead

into the stark,
unextraordinary cemetery...,
and everyone follows suit,
treading the same terrain over which
their ancestors were torn limb from limb.

Deliver my body from this body!,

deliver me
from memory!

For I've found second wind in this new blood, rigged
beyond recognition, sails in the breeze, and I'm arming it to the teeth.

1

Des civilisations ont basculé dans le vide
pour n'avoir pas su trouver à temps
le chemin
des terres belles te froufroutant au nez,
vieux déserteur !

Peuples sans haine et sans mesure,
boueux, très souriants
dans l'ovale opalin des terreurs rétrécies...

Ils avaient pour eux le temps, ils fouaillaient
dans l'espace, mais rien
n'éclata les libérant du gri-gri fumeux. Rien
qu'on vît s'aveuglant en éclipse...

1

Some civilizations have toppled into obscurity
for not having been able to follow, in a timely manner,
the way
to beautiful lands that were right under your nose,
old deserter!

Peoples devoid of hatred, immeasurable,
filthy, smiling ear-to-ear
in the opaline oval of narrowing terrors…

They had time all to themselves, they leafed
through space, but nothing
broke out to free them from the hazy gris-gris. The nothing
that one beholds, blinded by an eclipse...

AU PAYS DES MULTIFACES
à Brahim et Fatem

Parvenu au pays des Multifaces, qu'est-ce que je vois sinon un grouillement de corps enflés qui errent à l'aveuglette, foulent une peau d'hommes incapables de se tenir debout et en silence dans le désordre furieux de la cité.

Certains êtres, mêmes les chats, sont si maigres qu'on s'en détourne tant la férocité de leur déchaînement rappelle les clous qui fixèrent le Christ à la croix.

Peu de douceur donc dans cet oubli rocailleux et peu, très peu d'eau sauf par endroits la flaque sèche d'un nuage blanc.

C'est ici que l'enfer biblique s'ordonne à merci :

miroir à l'intérieur de quoi se désintègrent les fossiles vivants, errant le long des routes, dans les fossés, traversant les routes, poudreux et haillonneux.

Les Multifaces les méprisent, les craignent ; ils édifient partout où ils les voient des murs de silence. Ils les font parfois travailler sous la contrainte sans les payer. "On les nourrit, c'est déjà beaucoup, disent-ils."

Les Multifaces sont des voleurs et des inquiets mais leur inquiétude n'a rien d'honorable ; elle ne sécrète que le malheur des autres. Elle en tire son essence, s'en gave et l'entretient donnant elle-même dans la pire délinquance, ce qu'elle réprime le plus durement dans le comportement de la piétaille, chair ambulante.

Quand les Multifaces s'en prennent à leurs ancêtres, ils affûtent des haches et des couteaux et retirent de coffres de bois anciens des rouleaux de papier où sont inscrits des noms et des toponymes mystérieux. Ils vous livrent cela

IN THE COUNTRY OF MULTIFACES
for Brahim and Fatèm

Having landed in the country of the Multifaces, what's the first thing I see?: a swarm of swollen corpses, wandering around, blindly, treading the flesh of men incapable of rising to their feet during a moment of calm, surrounded by the disorder of the city, boiling over with fury.

Some creatures, even the cats, are so malnourished that it forces one's head to spin, swiftly, in the other direction, away from their sickly, emaciated skeletal frame, reminiscent of the very nails that once fixed Christ to the cross.

There is little gentleness to be found in this stone-strewn oblivion, and little, very little water, save for a few dry puddles, here and there, of colorless haze.

From here, Hell shouts its orders:

out of a mirror thriving with living and breathing and disintegrating fossils, a few errant stragglers moving out and about into the open streets, making their way down into the trenches, along the roads, dusty, run-down.

The Multifaces detest them, fear them; they build up towering walls of silence wherever they go. Sometimes they put them to work against their will, without pay: "We keep them clothed and fed, isn't that more than enough?" They make a habit of saying this.

The Multifaces are thieves and misanthropes, but there is no honor to be found in their brand of misanthropy; it merely secretes the misfortune of others. It derives its essence from it, feeds on and looks after it, gives itself over to the worst sorts of delinquency, which it tries its best to repress, to bury in its rank-and-file, its formless, vagrant flesh.

When the Multifaces take on their ancestors, they sharpen axes and knives and pull out scrolls of paper, inscribed with mysterious names and top-onyms, from ancient wooden coffers. A scribbled mess of arbitrary nonsense they

en vrac comme étant leur histoire, mais ils précisent d'emblée qu'ils n'ont pas d'ancêtre : "Je n'ai ni père ni mère, je suis autonome ; deux singes ont copulé sur une vieille branche et me voilà."

pass down to you, playing it off as their history, while claiming from the outset that they have no ancestor: "I have no father, no mother, I am autonomous; two monkeys copulated in a tree; and there you have it, here I am."

SIMBA

L'oripeau brûlait le vent ; le gel
incendiait la nuit — nos femmes
éclaboussaient le typhon...

Illuminé d'illusions brutales, tu portes
mon sang au bréchet noir de l'éclair...
Que la silice intente une ritournelle amère
au traceur du sillon
comme un stigmate sur le sein bleu des madones !

L'épervier fugace intente ses flagelles
à tes yeux épars, simba
quand je rugis, tueur,
en ce ciel urticant,
fléché au petit jour.

Je t'y remise, basilic très éprouvé, oblique
en la tornade pierreuse
entre l'iris et le ruisseau d'améthystes.

Lycaon, retourne au plus touffu de la glèbe !
regarde ton corps
amoureux de mains fourbies
par l'orage assassin.

Tu portes l'anneau d'or autour de tes chevilles
et la terre en carcan ;
écoute
le chagrin des termitières
et le soc aguerri surgi d'hélianthes
comme un rhizome au fond
des pupilles entrouvertes
à toi simba hué, tiré

SIMBA

A golden luster burned its way up the wind; the frost
was fanning the night's flame—our wives
circulating the waters of the typhoon...

Illuminated by brutal illusions, you heave
my blood into the blackened keel of lightning...
May the silica pursue its bitter refrain
through the tracing furrow,
like a scar across the blue, blue breast of the Madonna!

I let out my roar, O simba,
O killer; may it soar the urticant heavens
trailblazed by dawn's early light,
the fleeting, ephemeral hawk pursuing its flagella
through your disjointed eyes.

I stop you cold: a blighted, oblique basilisk,
in the rock-ribbed tornado,
between the iris and free-flowing amethyst.

Lycaon, take yourself back to the deepest of glebes!,
just look at you,
hopelessly in love with whose hands the tempests
have polished.

Around your ankles you wear a ring of gold,
the fettered land;
listen
to the woe of the termite mounds
and the season-polished plow, rising like a rhizome
from the sunflowers, the abyssal
and half-opened pupils
headed in your direction, O simba, skewered

par le Masaï buveur de lymphe !

vieux Masaï crépusculaire, tu entonnes :
"A jamais mort en moi le fauve aigri
ruisselant de sisal et de savanes,
car je reprends mes cauris au soleil dur !"

Dans mon cœur ton cœur pétille,
orchidée claire,
rampé de lunes, fourni d'ictère,
mustang hennissant en ellipse ordinaire
frémissante d'étoiles...
Basma brandie en style dru des tonnerres
sur une terre absente.

by Maasai, guzzlers of lymphatic fluid!,

the old crepuscular Maasai, sing out O Maasai, sing out:
"The cruel beast in me, rushing from the sisal,
from the savannahs, is forever undone,
for I have laid my cowry shells out in the unforgiving sunlight!"

Writhing with moons, lush with icterus,
O lit-up orchid,
your heart shines out from my heart,
like a mustang whose whinnying is an everyday ellipsis,
quivering in the starlight…
Basma brandishing the profusely stylistic thunders
over an absent land.

CARIE

à Zhor and Mustapha Iznasni

Chantant parmi toi, soleil précaire,
au-dessus des temps neufs
très mal conçus...
et dans tes cordes, mère
épouvantée d'arachnides...

aussi tremblant qu'un sol
en déroute sous le champ magnétique de la Terre,
je vois au fond tourbillonner, sinistre,
le demi-dieu, auteur des mers.

Je te démonte, t'assèche, sein gonflé de mûres,
de zinnias où ni la soie ni l'or
n'extraient
de mon silence la carie.

C'est le lait sué des sangs hideux,
le lait bleu des galaxies
que l'euphorbe et la ciguë remisent
en ton chant pétrifié.

Oiseau, ceins-moi d'abois, de sangles !
donne à mes yeux l'eau frémie, l'ombre
que déterrent
ces enfants haïs par l'ère.

DECAY

for Zhor and Mustapha Iznasni

Surrounding you with song, precarious sun,
over the poorly-conceived
times of ours...,
inside your vocal cords: my mother,
terrorized by arachnids...,

trembling like the soil
running beneath the Earth's magnetic field,
I stare down into the depths and see that ominous
demi-god, author of all seas, whirling.

I strip you down, dry you out, breast swollen like a blackberry,
like a zinnia where neither silk nor gold
extracts
senescence from my silence.

This is the milk, oozing from hideous bloodlines,
the blue milk that moves through galaxies,
stored away in your petrified song
by euphorbia and hemlock.

O bird, girdle me with your shrieks, restrain me!,
cast the ripples of the water before my eyes, the shadow
to disentomb
these children, despised by an era.

AÉROBIE

S'aérer, saut d'onces dans les yeux clairs de l'oryx ;
acacia turbulent, baobab chanteur, voici le don
du grand ruissellement...
Ah ! s'ennoblir de cette lune décrite
par le banjo crépusculaire assis
sur mes genoux et qui me parle
d'un temps de menthe et d'euphorbe...

Il suscite un Soleil absolu dans la ride
des astres et de l'éclipse...
La roue solitaire du paon blanc...
et mes larmes vitrioleuses.
Connaîtras-tu jamais ce cœur lucide,
sans abri, mené en palanquin :
rouleau barreur, éternité d'astéroïdes
ceignant l'Univers d'un regard nonpareil ?

Rêves au corps à corps tués et qui moisissent
à la lucarne du Néant...
c'est le fourmilion
sous un caroubier dit par le naja sonné sonnant
la nuit cousue de peaux de chiens,
c'est la muraille d'infra-sons
qui danse dans le vent magnétique en aiguilles.

Silence clairvoyant, princesse aimée
comme un scintillement d'eaux, de rocs et de sangs.

AEROBICS

To be the air's, the leopard's leap through the crystal eyes of the oryx;
the turbulent acacia, the singing baobab: this is the gift
of the great continuous stream...
Ah!, the ennoblement of this moon, outlined
by the twilight-inflected banjo resting
across my lap, conversing with me
over a time flourishing with mint, with euphorbia...

Rousing, from the shriveled skin of stars and eclipses,
one absolute Sun...
The solitary wheel of the colorless peacock...
and my vitriolic tears.
Will you ever really know this lucid, refuge-less
heart, conducted by palanquin:
the helmsman of a coxswain, an eternity of asteroids
encircling the entirety of the Universe with one unequivocal gaze?

Bodily dreams traversing the laid-waste bodies, rotting away
in the skylight of Nothingness...,
the ant lion
under the carob trees means the unsound naja will sound
the evening-woven hour from the flesh of dogs,
a mosaic of infra-sounds
dancing their way into magnetic winds, into needles.

The clairvoyant silence, the princess beloved
as light, glistening against water, across boulders and blood.

FIBULE

à Abdallah Stouky

Eucalyptus dessillant l'œil de l'aigle
taraudé d'ailes
où l'agrafe des protons s'ouvre
illuminant
les migrations lacustres... Longue,

longue est la rivière souveraine
tourmentée de soleil, surmontée d'arbres,
de monts
très lagunaires. Ici,
dérape la terre

— sur tes segments vernaculaires,
oiseau sans trille et sans aurore !
tu bruis au fond des mots usés, tu flambes
la galaxie radiée —
fantomale migratrice.

Eucalyptus que le corbeau incise
en orage pétillant
dans l'aiguille de midi.

Je martèle ma tête, le galet rouge
gros de vents et de mica
dans le lit du torrent asséché par tes yeux.

FIBULA

for Abdallah Stouky

The eucalyptus, peeling open the eye of the eagle
internally-threaded by wings,
from whose insides the staple of protons get pried open,
illuminating
the ever-lacustrine migrations…Long,

long is the sovereign river,
tormented by sun, surmounted by trees,
by lagoon-
laden mountains. Here,
the earth loses step

—over your vernacular parapets, O bird,
O trill-less, aurora-less bird!
you murmur from the depths of worn-out words, wrap
the galaxy, radiant, in burning flames—
phantasmal migrator.

The eucalyptus, wrested out by a crow,
into a sparkling tornado
along the sharpened edge of noon.

I beat my fists against my head, a red pebble
rounded by winds and mica,
down in the torrent's bed left high and dry by your eyes.

L' EUPHORBE

Je brûlerai ton or avec mes yeux,
Je cacherai ton cœur dans ma peau...

Il y a des galets sûrs...(Assour
bombardée du silence éternel...)

Il y a l'enfantement en pièces !...
et à l'entour des trottoirs
l'arrangement,
un vaste entendement...

Œil sans exemple, assois ta mort coquette
dans le chas d'une aiguille !
va ! tu vas, mais tu reviens,
couchée en l'herbe qu'infirme
la dent bleue du Soleil.

Va ! tu es toujours ici, assise
et blanche,
roulant la béquille du Torrent sans merci,
me retenant
dans tes serres fortes et solennelles
avec...
Quoi ? Dis-moi quoi ? Veux-tu
que j'aille au diable ?

Ici, ni mort ni vie, hormis
cette arlequine vie ! Ici,
c'est le sable qui pense...

Amour ! Amour ! Je vois
crier les vieilles images.

THE EUPHORBIA

With my eyes, I will burn away your gold;
in my skin, I will bury your heart...

Look—out there are pebbles; steadfast, sure... (Assur,
bombarded by eternal silence...)

Look—out there is creation, in pieces!...,
lingering about the sidewalks,
an alliance,
one vast compliance...

O Eye without Equal, slip your death,
your coquettish death, through the eye of its needle!,
Get lost!, go, though I know you will swing back,
sinking deep into the grass, quashed
by the Sun's blue tooth.

Get lost! Why do you sit there so,
ghostly,
spinning the Torrent's crutch, mercilessly,
holding me back
with your strong and solemn talons,
with...
What? Tell me, what are you waiting for? For me
to pave my way to hell?

Here; deathless, lifeless: outside
a harlequin's stare! Here, where
sands are swelling with thought ...

Love! O Love! I can see
the old images crying out.

Que revienne l'Astre inouï supputant
"que tout est autre chose" !
Que revienne donc cet Astre décrié ;
je suis assis
dans la criée des morts
et dans le Livre.

Rien, jamais rien n'étranglera l'Euphorbe!

May the unknown Star swing back around, proposing
"that all is altogether something else!"
May this outcast of a Star swing back around;
I have sunk myself
into the sulking of dead men,
alongside the Book.

Nothing, absolutely nothing, will drown out the Euphorbia!

SOMMEIL MÉGALITHIQUE

Mon Dieu ! Donnez-lui donc la fleur parfaite
du Soleil.
L'éventail chatoyant du colibri
Comme le vit l'enfant inculquant aux cimes le bec
incident des tectoniques...

Tu marches dans mon sommeil en mégalithe, abattant
autour des éternels courriers la peur
qui difforme ces peuples...

La Nuit les brise en bubons noirs
sur les arêtes du Temps !
Les fend en involucres sur les dents
du Lycaon
extracteur de la Mort
de la Savane où court mon bel Oryx.

Soleil contigu aux mers parfaites
des nébuleuses !

Zhor ! Lorsque tu eus franchi les Sept portes, tu me dis :
"J'ai brûlé l'Ombre Amère ! Désormais seuls compteront
les Sept Grains du Collier."

A travers toi sifflaient les traverses du vent,
l'oléandre des rivières s'inventa oiseau bleu ;
l'éclair mourut entre tes doigts ;
les sédiments mal inscrits corrigèrent la montagne
et glissèrent, formidables et solennels — errants —
sous la peau des Tantales...

Les madrépores, les actinies longuement épelées ;
la surface intempestive de la mort

MEGALITHIC SLEEP

My God! Just do it, give up your Sun-perfected
flower already.
The hummingbird's lustrous fan,
through the eyes of a child, instilling the peaks with the tectonics
of unexpected beaks…

You make your way through my megalithic sleep, sweeping
over eternal couriers the fearful winds
deforming these peoples…

Night breaks them into black buboes
against the outer limits of Time!
Splits them into involucres between the teeth
of the Lycaon,
extractor of Death,
through whose Savannah my sweet Oryx is racing.

Sun running off into the nebulae's
unequalled seas!

Zhor! Once you made it through the Seven gates, you said to me
"I have burned the Bitter Shadow! Henceforth shall recognize
only the Seven Seeds of the Necklace."

It's through you that the crosswinds whistled,
the riverside's oleander dreamed itself up a blue, blue bird;
the lightning passed through your fingers and perished;
the impressions of the sediment repositioned the mountain,
and slid, wondrously, solemnly—errantly—
under the skin of the Tantaluses…

The madrepores, the sea anemones extensively spelled out;
the unpropitious surface of death

en cauris cinglés de seins, de hanches,
ceinte de la peau lisse des ténèbres ;
le baobab debout dans les calamités,
témoin des drames anciens ;
la piste de marbre et le dos roui d'étoiles
délétères
fouettant sur la rocaille l'esclave amer.

Il se peut qu'un ancêtre ait mal compris le parler clair
de la Terre !
et que je sois ensauvagé, grinçant avec
les modules de mes enfances rôdeuses !

Mais non !
Mais si !

Accroché à tes veinules, je suis celui
qui pagaie et qui t'aime.

wrought from cowry shells, clinging to hips, breasts, and thighs,
girdled by the shadows' smooth skin;
the baobab looming over the cataclysms,
witness to ancient dramas;
the marbled pathway and retted spine of the stars
slipped loose,
whipping the bitter slave into the gravel.

It's possible that some ancestor misconstrued the clear speech
of the Earth!,
that I am made to be savage, squealing with
the magnitude of my lowly youth!

No, no!
Oh, but yes!

Lashed to your every venule, I am he
who pledges to row, to love you.

SCORPION
à Paul Dakeyo

Avec ton œil-lamie éclaboussant le soleil,
scorpion attaché au néant par ton dard ;
avec tes armes, laminaire,
scorpion debout et fort
au creux de la vague de mon sang mâle et sale ;

C'est avec ton crochet, c'est avec ton stigmate,
agités dans la nuit ;
c'est avec ta voix contuse, avec
la prose inerte de ton venin
qu'oublié parmi moi se lèvera le Sommeil ;

Scorpion ! Scorpion ! Batouque
d'asthénies assagies en la ténèbre précaire ;
lamentable, tu tiens Orphée avec
l'Arc-en-ciel ordinaire ;
scorpion, tu tiens l'Erreur.

Tu vidas mon corps du vieux suaire,
ma peau était claire, mon sang claquait
aux javelles, aux javelines, ô Noir dicté
à l'Or fascinateur,
à la mortelle saison ;

Je suis un astre qui corrige
l'Alpha et l'Oméga, l'étrange sort
de l'échelle éperdue qui ne connut de la Lune
que le piquet des salves lointaines ;
fontes, robots et morts

Assis en mon œil éclaté par l'éclair ;
éther jonglé, champ d'armes pures,

SCORPION

for Paul Dakeyo

With your porbeagle-eye, whipping the sun's light about,
O scorpion, your stinger clinging to oblivion;
along with your arsenals and your laminaria,
flourishing, O determined scorpion,
from the crests of my bloody waves, brutish and filthy;

And along with your hook, along with your spiracle,
spiraling throughout the night,
And along with your wound of a voice, and your
venom's inert prose,
unbeknownst to me, traveling the upswells of Sleep;

Scorpion! O scorpion! The bouts of asthenia
in this batuque assuage such precarious shadows from within;
inconsolable, you grasp at Orpheus with
your prosaic rainbow;
O scorpion, what you grasp at is Errata.

How, from my body you've drained the old shroud,
my skin so crystalline, my blood whistling
into sheaves, javelins, O Blackness dictated
to the dazzling Gold,
the ghastly season;

I am just an astral body, ameliorating
the Alpha and the Omega, the strange destiny
of a boundless scale whose only conception of the Moon
remains the measures of salvos in the distance;
fonts, robots, and death

nestled within my eye, extracted by the lightning's excisions;
the juggled aether, a landscape of absolute munitions,

ficelé et tuant à merci l'Arachnide
en ton crochet avec les Sept grains de poison,
Scorpion, qui es-tu ?

— Je ne suis qu'une salve !
Une berbère et une salve.
Or me voici bleue-noire,
arthropode géante,
ô nain, ô nègre, me voici

avec mes philtres, avec mon rire,
totem, ô noir totem !
je suis la scorpionne qui erras
sur ta peau assassine,
jujubier mal entendu ;

il est dans le puits un sourire d'enfant
que tu ne me fis pas ;
le bidon, le bidonville au fond du puits éclaire
le frétillement des étoiles tirées à blanc ;
il est dans ma vie noire

un éclat de vaisselle ;
semonce à l'Apode élancé, semonce à l'Aube,
ô Nuit ! Semonce !
diamant réfractaire aboli par mon œil
dans l'eau cassée d'arums !

C'est au fond des cryptes que je mesure à l'envers
du désastre ta ride ;
c'est au fond de la craie et de ce tableau noir
que mes orteils retracent
le chemin creux des vies errantes ; au fond
très lapidaire de mes pupilles

strung together to lay mercilessly waste the sole Arachnid
dwelling inside your hook, with its Seven seedlings of poison,
Scorpion, who are you?

—I am no more than a salvo!,
The salvo of an Amazigh.
Gaze upon my black-and-blue,
my gigantic arthropodic body,
O dwarf, O negro, here I come,

with my potion, my totemic
laughter, O totem of darkness!,
I am the scorpion, meandering
across your murderous skin,
O misconstrued jujube tree;

from the well comes the smile of a child
that wasn't made to fit me;
the slum, the slums at the bottom of the well that illuminate
the wriggling, white-hot stars that shoot their blanks;
from the darkness of my life

comes a glow of earthenware;
take warning willowy Apode, take warning O Dawn,
O Night! Take warning!,
obstinate diamond that my eye abolishes
as it emerges from the lily-broken water!

From the deepest crypts, from the opposing side of devastation,
I size up your shriveled skin.
From the depths of this chalky dust, upon this black tablet
my feet trace out
the gaunt paths of errant lives; from the deepest lapidary
depths of my pupils

que je te vois couché, lion simple, once d'or...
— J'étais l'enfant abominable, l'enfant
qui jouait sous le figuier avec Bételgeuse
vibrionnaire, maléfique
et porté parmi le sel aux négresses qui cisaillèrent

mon front, mes tempes !
il n'est de nuit que toi qui marches en mes replis ;
il n'est de mort venue que de toi, scorpionne ;
car tu es la marelle,
l'intelligence et la marelle.

Tu me verras sculpté en scapulaire autour du cou
des vigognes et des gargouilles ; autour du cou
des dromadaires et des cigognes... Essaim
brimé d'arrois ailés ; tu me verras sur le coup
de midi brisant la Mer.

Nous l'avons enchantée avec notre rosaire ;
c'est avec ma voix, ta voix, avec le cri d'Eole
que nous bâtîmes autour d'elle cet arbre mirifique ;
elle eut à nous dire, elle eut à nous décrire
alors que la nuit consommait le Soleil
gisant — apothéose !

dans le cœur même des crocodiles — ;
Souïmangas battant le cimier buffle collinaire
qui me couvrez du manteau et du pleur sarrasin !
quand mon sang terre rougie sans couchant et sans aurore,
affine l'osselet du dinosaure ;

quand ma tête décodée sculpta l'hypogée ; quand
tout mon or ruissela,
ô nuit,
dans son sourire ;

where I find you nestled, O level-headed lion, leopard of gold…
—I was an abominable child, a child who
under the fig tree would while away the hours
alongside the vibrant and maleficent Betelgeuse,
before being washed out to sea, to the negresses,

who cut my brow and my temples down to size!
Come night, nothing but you will make its way into my downturns:
nothing but death itself, circling its way back to you, O scorpion;
for hopscotch becomes you,
slyness and hopscotch.

You will find me sculpted into scapulary, around the neck
of every vicuna and every gargoyle; around the neck
of every camel, around the neck of every stork…A whirlwind,
downtrodden by wingèd arrows; you will find me at the stroke
of noon, parting the open Sea.

It was we who enchanted it with our rosary;
with my voice, your voice, the cry of Aeolus,
who erected this marvelous tree;
and it spoke to us, it spoke to us in detail,
as the night consumed the recumbent
Sun—of apotheosis!,

an apotheosis buried in the heart of crocodiles—;
The souimangas unfurled their wings over the hilly buffalo crest
wrapping me up in its overcoat and its weepy buckwheat!,
as my earthly blood grew deeper red, without the glow of rising or setting suns,
and Jurassic bones continued to churn beneath the soil;

as my decrypted skull sculpted the hypogaeum; as
all my gold flowed out,
O night,
into its smile;

il n'est qu'un cheval fou pour émonder l'arbuste,
il n'est

qu'un roulis calme
pour déliter l'îlot guerrier ! Sumer,
il n'est qu'une muraille excitée par l'abeille-memnon,
fleuve habillé de ciels contus
vers ma tombe souveraine...

Il n'est que ce quignon, Joseph, il n'est que cette coupe
vide et pourtant remplie en son vide par mon pleur,
écrasement du rouleau sur la grève où pense le Mort,
Batouque !

Batouque ! il n'est de clair, ô stégomyie, Pharos !
que le marbre ébranlé très suicideur, bâti,
sans socle bâti
sur la Ténèbre délétère,
Batouque

de grisaille vêtue et de corail tueur —
Le Combattant Suprême est mort, voici
l'affaire punique !
Un chien, un très vieux chien redéterre mes os —,
Le Combattant Suprême est mort.

— A mort tous les oiseaux d'augure !
Je suis l'enfant du Lotophage,
la datte et le lotus,
un vrai soleil levant ;
mais pas l'étrange démon coupé, cassé, l'étrange

absolution ; je suis
le séné et la férule,
la particule in extremis visible en la cornée

until nothing was left but a mad horse left pruning the shrubs,
nothing more

than a gently rolling wave
to erode the soldiering islet! O Sumer,
nothing but a fortification roused by the Memnon-bee,
O river robed in heavenly wounds
making its way toward my sovereign tomb…

Nothing but this crust, Joseph, nothing but this emptied
vessel, nevertheless overflowing with my empty weeping,
a rolling crush against the shoreline where Death reflects,
Batuque!

Batuque!, there's nothing so clear, O stegomyiae, O Pharos!,
as the undermining of the openly suicidal marble, erected
without foundation, erected
upon disintegrating Shadow,
Batuque,

vested by the grisaille and deadly coral—
The Supreme Combatant is dead: behold
this Punic affair!
A dog, some age-old dog, is unearthing my bones yet again—,
The Supreme Combatant is dead.

—Death to all these ominous birds!
I am child of the Lotophagus,
the date, and the lotus,
the true sun, rising;
but not this strange demon, out of touch, broken, this strange

absolution; I am
the senna, the ferula,
the visible particle in extremis within the cornea,

qui n'est que serres
du rouleau démembré par le bec des pygargues...

Je suis le pain et le levain,
le vin,
l'Alpha et l'Oméga,
mais voici qu'autour de moi
danse le scorpion !

which are but talons
of the scroll, picked apart by the beaks of eagles...

I am the bread and the levain,
the wine,
the Alpha and the Omega,
and still, whipping itself around me,
the scorpion dances!

REAGAN-PISTOLEROS

L'armée est nue
nulle et non avenue ;
chacun ondoie dans la nuit ;
et le vieillard inepte,
redevenu cruel comme l'enfant qu'il était,
frappe et refrappe
sur tous les vieux tombeaux
tendus en cercle sur le brouillard
du matin atomique ;

Où sont tes vieux jeux, tueur fébrile ?
où est ta langue, crocodile ?
et que dis-tu de la Mare Nostra ?
— je la brûle !
je brûle à ma guise cet entendement,
et ce Congrès qui n'est qu'un vieux chiffon véreux !
je suis le cow-boy élu par les étoiles ;
et mal luné, je tue l'Arabe,
et, traître, je rejoue
un vieux western grinçant,
et puis on me pendra.

Nixon était un homme formidable qui sut
tout mettre de côté, les êtres et les choses ;
il régla le conflit atroce du Viêt-nam
en allant lui-même saluer le Poète
Mao ;

Il empêcha toute guerre de n'être qu'un horizon
de rapières, d'immenses gerbes d'or
que compulse le Temps ;

mais toi, Reagan, qui es-tu ? Dis-nous pourquoi

REAGAN-PISTOLEROS

The army, exposed,
void, becomes a requisite avoidance;
as evening falls, every last one begins to waver;
and the old man, inept
and cruel as he was back in his youth,
beats again and again,
against the doors of mournful tombs
fanned out into a circle, amid the hazy mist
of atomic morning;

Hot-headed murderer, what old tricks are you up to?,
cat got your tongue, O crocodilian thing?,
how about that Mare Nostrum?
—I'll burn it!,
I'll burn, as I please, your reason to the ground,
along with that Congress, that worm-eaten rag!,
I go by the name cowboy-chosen-by-the-stars;
moon-mad, I plot my assassinations of Arabs
before, feverish with treason, I play out
that old overplayed western,
before I'm hanged.

Nixon, what a formidable man, someone who really knew
how to sweep everything aside, beings and things;
that atrocious Vietnam conflict—sorted it out
nicely, all while saluting Mao,
Supreme Poet;

He stopped every war before it turned into a horizon
of rapiers, into immense sweeps of gold
compelled by time;

but you, Reagan, what are you? And why,

t'attaques-tu au Silence éternel, au soleil ?
Tu n'es que le cuir chevelu du Sommeil
humain ! je te déserte.

O — Pas de déportation !
kaf
Il n'est de clair ici que le sabot de l'onagre
et l'étincelle des galaxies et l'or noir intenté
à ma prière abandonnée, charogne,

O grain de sable, sais-tu
que je te suis préexistant ?

Je suis l'Ecarlate qui mesure l'Espace
et l'or goulu que tu insultes.

why are you so quick to lash out at the Eternal Silence, at the sun?
Nothing but the shaved head of human Sleep,
that's what you are! And I forsake you.

O—steps of deportation!,
kaf,
There is nothing so clear as the onager's hoof,
the sparkling of galaxies, or the black gold laid
before my prayer, left in the dust, O carrion,

O grain of sand, don't you understand
that my existences precedes yours?

I am that Scarlet, that tracing of Space,
and the gluttonous gold that you've degraded.

FLORILÈGE DU PRINTEMPS MAUDIT
à Claude Bonnefoy

Je suis assis par là, sanglé de vieux trachomes...
Debout, parfois debout cinglé du rire tuant !

Je caresse le galet, l'hyperbole et le chaos
et ses cheveux avec mes éclairs contigus

à l'hysope et au sable enviés en sourdine...
Allez ! Battez-vous, chiens vulgaires, battez-vous !

Mais toi, là-bas, très juste, toi qui remues ma nuit,
avec tes miroirs, tes racines et tes cris...

Donne! Oh donne un peu de cet amour-cola!
Mots ajustés, sans arme, errant dans le corps roide !

Ni moi-même, égrené, concassé, démembré !
Donne ! Oh toi qui toujours donnes ! cette ombre

à nos langues perdues, à l'idiome aberrant.

*   *   *

Venu là par quel langage, bardé de sales étoiles...
— Eclipses amères ! Terreurs maniaques !
décrochés de mon temps, sordide et simple, je marche
sur les tisons du vieux sang clair.

L'acier pleure ! Le soleil atroce suppure
en ma tête, heurtant encore la mort
avec son aile d'oiseau faste que tu supprimes !

Je me tue et rebondis, je regarde les griffeurs.

FLORILEGIUM FOR THE CURSED SPRING

for Claude Bonnefoy

Driven into snares of old trachoma, I sit, inhabiting these whereabouts,
sometimes driven to my feet, driven mad by murderous laughter!

I run my hands over pebble, hyperbole, and chaos alike,
I run my hands through its hair, my lightning continuing

enviously into the hyssop, into the sands, into the silence…
Onward! Get fighting, you lowly, mangey dogs, get fighting!

But you, over there, so just, you who stir my night
with your every mirror, your every root, your every cry…

Give it up! Oh give up just one iota of that kola-adoration!
The tailored words, unarmed, wandering the rigid body!

Not I, shelled, ground to powder, dismembered!
Give it up! Oh you, forever giving!, give this shadow up

to our errant tongues, to the aberrant idiom.

*   *   *

Alighted from what language, ramshackled with filthy stars…
—Curdling eclipses!, maniacal terrors!,
unwoven from our sordid and simple era, as I go walking
the ashen remains of age-old, illumined blood.

The steel weeps! The atrocious sun festers
inside my head, hurtling toward Death,
Death, whose lavish wingspan you suppress!

I take my own life and spring right back, I gaze longingly at the claws.

Je m'enchante et me torture, je vois bien que tu n'es là,
fantôme des objets éclatants, que tu ne passes

qu'avec mon oubli sous l'aisselle et ma tête,
mon être liminaire et les roches ardentes !
Homme venu du grain monumental du vide.

*   *   *

Où que tu ailles, ton corps se dissocie de toi,
il incendie la ville déjà morte d'elle-même !

Où que te portent tes jambes dissemblables, mais coi !
ramassé sur toi seul en cerceau de terreurs !

je joue à te griller la prunelle et je frappe
de cécité l'idiot complice qui nous divulgue !

Tu paies d'une haine incalculable le sang
de ton sang versé là sous des bris de sourires.

Et tu manges des morts et tu mâches des balles...
Et tu vieillis plus vite que l'ancien crépuscule !

En mon cœur, c'est la poudre innommée qui titube
sachant qu'à tuer le ciel se brise avec

nos larmes assassines et nos doutes vacants !
Tes ancêtres te renient, mais je suis encore ici !

*   *   *

J'arpentais ton visage convulsé en tonnerres !
J'arpentais cette terre, je me voyais — vieux hère — effleurer
l'arbre et l'ange, retourner à l'arbre cher !

I delight and torture myself, I see that you aren't there,
O ghost of glowing objects, that you continue on your way,

this oblivion of mine tucked under your arm, along with my head,
along with my liminal being, and all those ardent rocks of yours!
Man, alighted from the monumental seed of the void.

*   *   *

Wherever you go, your body dissociates,
burning down the already-dead city it is!

Wherever your lospsided legs carry you, sweeping you up,
however serene it may seem, into a sort of cyclical terror!

—whatever complicit idiot might give us away,
I strike him blind, I turn your pupil over this rotisserie!

For your blood, you pay with immeasurable hatred,
your own blood poured out, under cracking smiles.

And you devour the dead, and you chew the bullets…
And you age faster than the timeless twilight itself!

And my heart, it's a wavering, unknowable dust
that knows: Any undoing of the heavens means subduing

our murderous tears and our empty-headed doubts!
Your ancestors may desert you, but I'm not going anywhere!

*   *   *

I strode through the storming forks of your face!
I strode that land, and I saw myself—an old wretch—grazing
the trees and the angels, return to that beloved tree!

Il ne pointe de là qu'un vieux doigt qui menace ;
eux vivent et grondent ! Le bigorneau est mort !
Je passe sans cortège, sans éclat, sans délire.

Folie ! Folie ! Détachons-les
de cette terre !
Entrons dans l'éclair solennel qui m'amenuise !

Réapprenons le mot simple qui me déchire !
Parce que le soleil dans sa couronne de pus
comme un archer debout sur mon corps voit ailleurs

se mouvoir mon errance et se distordre mon ombre
qui n'est que le feu clairvoyant, l'écume amère !
Oh ! mon enfant donne ! Donne au vieux, bougeant la tête,

la lumière insaisissable de tes yeux que je hante !

From there, he directs your eye with one single, sinister finger;
these people: they are living still, still rumbling! The periwinkle has died!
I pass by, devoid of any procession, glow, or deliriousness.

Madness! Madness! Let's unleash them
from this land!
Let's enter into the lightning, the solemn lightning that wears me away!

Let's relearn what undoes me: the word, unadorned!
Because the sun, crowned in its pus,
looms over my body like an archer, watching my restlessly

wandering body from afar, and my shadow grow more and more disfigured,
this shadow of mine: clairvoyant fire, bitter scum!
Oh! Yield, my child! Yield to this old man, whose head motions toward you

the unseizable light of your eyes, those very hollows that I haunt!

CONTRETEMPS

Mais qu'il vienne et tourne, tourne ce pur séisme
autour de toi avec ses ceintures de crotales !
Que la Terre obscurcie par mon cœur épandu
sur les vertèbres du ciel irradie l'ocelle qu'arrache
sauvagement de l'épeire ton œil fœtal !

Démembré, reculant et comptant, démembré,
assis sur les stupres et trahi, assis sur l'ange
cruel qui n'est qu'une affre ! assis
sur moi riant et pleurant ce monde qui meurt...
O chair ! emporte dans mes rides le soleil !

Venu là oh ! quelle ombre ! oh quelle fiente !
venu là avec ce qui s'en va, cruellement précaire,
foi cachée sous l'angoisse tutélaire...
Qu'il advienne donc la pire mort !

Mais nous autres assis, debout, braquant sur ordre,
sans jeu regardant jongler prophètes et terres !
nous autres crevés sous la dent du lycaon,
cassés, réprimés, crachant le lait des mères !

Tu meurs ! Tu meurs ! Qu'on en finisse !
Va-t-en ! Va-t-en ! Qu'on en finisse !

CONTRETEMPS

But may it close back in on and encircle you, encircle you
with the pure seismicity of cinched-together rattlesnakes!,
May the Earth grow obscured by my heart, stretched
across the heavenly vertebrae, illuminating the ocellus
that savagely wrests from the orb weaver your faetal eye!

Dismembered, recoiling and reeling about, dismembered,
settling upon its stupors, and betrayed, planted over the cruelty
of angels whose only form is woe!, settling
upon myself; I, who laugh and weep over a dying world...
O flesh!, lug some sun into this shriveled skin of mine!

And so there arose, oh!, what shadow!, oh, what utter feces!,
and so there arose whatever comes only to go again: this secretive
faith, stowed away in tutelary anguish...
And may death follow with it, the absolute worst of death!

As for the rest of us, above and below, unconstrained, embattled
with law and order, eyeing the juggling acts of prophets and lands!,
as for the rest of us, we are crushed between the jaws of the Lycaon:
broken, repressed, mother's milk spewing from our open mouths!

Die, already, die! Die! May it finally play out, once and for all!
Get out of here! Out! May it finally play out, once and for all!

SUR LE TROTTOIR DU LIBAN

Quand il eut effilé l'or violent des roses, il alla
de fleur en fleur obséder le vieux rêve ;
et après s'être assis, roncier puissant,
dans les eaux grises de nos rougeoles,
il se gava du corps goulu, des croûtes hâlées
des terres sautées à blanc...

Ce fut l'amer savoir,
un grouillement d'ellipses :
chaque corps d'exil allant vers soi hurlant :
" Honni soit le silence et ses conspirations ! "

Il étala sur le rire émeutier sa peau bistre,
saupoudra nos peurs de poux griffeurs ;
il adjura la haine d'armer l'enfant
de rigoles de sang ;
toujours véloce, il emboucha
la trompette des morts...
et siffla dans la nuit de la strideur étrange
bousculant tes joies cousues d'escarres...

Corps brûlé, très solennel,
surgi d'oponces et d'escarbilles —
il ourdit, fourbit depuis le bleu de l'algue
l'épaisseur de nos ténèbres — ;
corps effilé, suint de l'or des roses :

"... Je conspuerai le miroir fauve,
j'arracherai tous les rhizomes,
travailleur du basalte en l'éclair assourdi ;
et j'inscrirai en faux ta mémoire pantelante..."
Béquille aux dents, vieux factionnaire,
tu glapis sur le trottoir du Liban...

190

ON A SIDEWALK IN LEBANON

Once the roses' violent gold had withered at his bequest, he went
from flower to flower, haunting the antiquity of the dream;
and after enthroning himself, this thorny thing,
in the gray waters of our rubeola,
he gorged himself on the over-bloated body, bronze scabs
of land sautéed into nothingness…

This was a bitter knowledge,
a whirlwind of ellipses:
each exiled body hurtling towards you, screaming:
"Woe to silence, to its conspiracies!"

He rolled his soot-brown skin over the riotous laughter,
sprinkled our fears with the lithe claws of lice;
he begged hate to dress the child
in rivulets of blood;
ever swift, he wrapped his lips
around the trumpet of the dead…
and blew a strange stridency into the night,
disquieting the nerves of your coarsely-woven joys…

A solemnly silent and burnt-up corpse
came spewing from the opuntia and ember-heavy clouds—
and he emerged from his shell, bearing the depths of our darkness
from the seaweed's blue—;
his body slender, oozing from the roses' gold:

"…I shall rain hatred upon the tawny mirror,
rip every last rhizome from the ground,
O layer of lightning-muted basalt;
and in bad faith I shall inscribe your breathless memory…"
Old sentinel, crutch in teeth,
how you go shrieking across the Lebanese sidewalk…

Mais c'est la meule autour d'un dieu houleux,
autour
de l'enfance éclatée, criblée, couchée
sur les gravats du ciel...

Atome souviens-toi ! Il fera jour afin
que cet enfant maudit joue avec une étoile.

Though it's the grindstone that surrounds a howling god,
surrounding
a wrecked, rag-tag childhood, spread out
across the sky's rubble...

Remember, O atom! Once the dawn breaks,
this accursed child will have a star to play with.

ESSAOUIRA

C'est le pays de la fleur éternelle et du murex
et c'est mon cœur ourlé des larmes noires du Soleil :
vertu du vent, galet brisé très désertique...

C'est le ciel assujetti à l'abyssale ellipse,
une terre tumescente...

C'est l'ombre et le périple d'Hannon
éclaboussant les quasars !

Voici la glaise cunéiforme,
le glaive, le javelot et l'aiguille ;
voici la toge écarlate et le cuir vert de l'île ;
c'est la prison libertaire ferrée à blanc,
la chaloupe de Charon :
nuage ! nuage !
à quand le grain marron ?
Et qui dira le thuya ?

ESSAOUIRA

Here we have the land of the eternal flower, of the murex,
and here we have my heart, hemmed-in via the black tears of the Sun:
the virtue of wind, the vastly ruptured desert rock...

Here we have the sky, subjected to abyssal ellipses,
a tumescent land...

Here we have the shadow, and the voyage of Hanno
splashing through the quasars!

And here we have the cuneiform clay,
the glaive, the javelin, and the needle;
and here we have the scarlet toga and the isle's green leather;
Here we have the libertarian prison, enchained to nothingness,
Charon's shallop:
Cloud!, O cloud!,
How long, exactly, before the seed goes brown?
And what will hang from the lips of thuja?

FASCINATION

C'est une fille de la nuit démesurée aux yeux de poulpe,
turbulente d'oiseaux que le grimoire réveille
en la veillée d'écrits qui moussent
à ta lèvre tempétueuse ;
c'est une fille endormie dans l'éclair bleu des vagues,

un regard d'enfant en larmes.
C'est un cahier d'écolier pourrissant dans la décharge,
poudreux d'orties, papillonnant de musiques ;
l'éclat de rire d'une fillette, le déferlement des vagues
comme une danse de brousse attisée par le ciel.

Fascinateur de la nuit miroitant de vieux mondes,
portant haut le rêve amer,
je te vois couché, cerclé de sol happés du sang
des morts,
lapidant le corps servile ;

tu es l'écrit qui parle du vent, d'abysses et d'or,
tu te consumes en l'aubier fort des tornades
qui s'évaporent de ton œil clair.
Malentendeur, debout ! Enoch, debout
dans la rosace, dans le rameau noir des étoiles !

FASCINATION

Here we have a lady of unfathomable night, with the eyes of an octopus,
birds, awoken by the grimoire, whirling about her
in the wake of written words that foam
from your tempestuous lips;
here we have a lady sleeping in the blue glow of the waves,

the gaze of a weeping child.
Here we have a schoolboy's notebook rotting away on the garbage heap,
swept over by nettles, fluttering with music;
a burst of laughter from a little girl, the breaking of waves
like a bush-dance brought into being by the heavens.

The fascination of night, sparkling with old worlds,
flying its curdled dream from airy heights,
I see you sprawled out, surrounded by soil intermingling with the blood
of the dead,
lambasting the servile corpse;

you are the script that speaks through wind, through abysses and gold,
you are consumed by the great sapwood of tornados
that evaporate from your crystalline eye.
Rise up, numbskull! Enoch, rise up
and into the rose window, into the starry black branch!

TRIDENT

"Or le dieu s'en était allé en une
terre lointaine chez les Ethiopiens
qui, aux extrémités du monde, sont
partagés en deux, les uns au
Couchant, les autres à l'Orient
d'Hypérion. "

- Homére (*L'Odyssée*)

Que d'écrit rien ne réprouve l'eau !
tu calmeras ces fondrières...

J'agite le tonnerre
et le silence du rémora.

Militant de songes casseurs de temps exclus,
à sec grimé de tétanies,
j'opère dans l'enfer du sel crié
en béryls, en atonies.

Mes larmes nettoient le Rift, assis,
debout, errant, très noir;
rageur et sûr ;
j'armerai l'éclair parfait
de phaétons maudits.

Que soit maudit qui dans mon œil vacille
en ergots de nuit très légendaire !
O sourire avachi par le miroir des gaves,
il est un autre jour où la rétine absolve
l'édit clair des ténèbres.

Mais je te vois miner l'éclat, le stylet dur

TRIDENT

> "And now the god had ventured into a
> faraway land, among the Ethiopians,
> who, at the far ends of the earth, are
> a people divided, some towards
> the Sunset, others East
> of Hyperion."
>
> - Homer (*The Odyssey*)

In writing, nothing dares to condemn the water!
May your calmness sweep over these swamps...

I let loose thunder,
and the silence of the remora.

Illusory soldiers, breakers of the atmosphere cast out,
dried-up, bleared over by tetanic seizures,
I do what I do from inside the salt of hell, screaming
through the beryl, through the atony.

My tears cleanse the Rift; I sit,
I stand, I wander, darkly,
self-assured and rageful;
Watch me as I arm the exquisite lightning
with doomed Phaethons.

May it be cursed, these innards encompassed by my eye, coursing
the mountain streams of everlasting night!
O smile, warped by the mirroring pools of mountain streams,
a new day is breaking, one whose retina absolves
the glowing edict of shadows.

Though still I watch you eat away the lightning, the hard stylus

des luminaires...
Mais je te vois mûrir en flambées pures,
Je te vois, désert frappé à blanc
feulant, cerclé d'oiseaux et de varans.

Je vous le dis, si mal lamé
de Cafrerie :
voici brandi l'or alarmé.
C'est l'éprouvette centrifuge,
le sourire amer du caelacanthe.

Il t'obnubile, nuit démente ;
vaste éclaireur, il te décompte,
armé d'absolution,
forclos, inerte ; mais dis-moi
le soleil bleu d'iris,
car je l'écris à l'arc sur le plasma mal dit
de l'écliptique, des fleurs et sur
mes lanternes éteintes.

of light...
though still I watch you swell into the purest of blazes.
I watch you, O desert, beaten down to nothingness,
howling, your birds and lizards encircling you.

I speak these words to you, loosely-fit with Kaffrarian
lamé:
what you see is the raised specter of startled gold.
The centrifugal eprouvette,
the bitter smile of coelacanth.

It overwhelms you, O dementia-ridden night;
O far-reaching scout, how it surveys you,
armed with absolution,
foreclosed, unmoving; still, speak to me
of that iris-blue sun,
so that I might scrawl its arc over the crawling phrase
of ecliptic plasma, over the flowers, over
the dying light of my lanterns.

IN MEMORIAM

Hind !
C'est à l'autre bout de la nuit que le désert
nivelle
une fragmentation d'étoiles natives dont chaque
battement exsude une myriade de vies errantes...

Il n'est ni l'Hadès ni même le Cocyte,
mais une irisation d'eaux
que tes yeux enflamment en gentianes
sur un miroir où le ciel prend son bain de cygne fauve...

Des dieux au cimier flamboyant te voient venir du fond
des cataclysmes éternels,
portant entre tes doigts les vrais signes de la Terre
et l'écrit indomptable qui filigrane ton âme...

Ils forment une haie souveraine à ton approche...
au-dessus de leurs casques
tourbillonnent les ailes des vieux démons...

Ils libèrent dans un souffle irradiant
des colombes aussi blanches que les opales laiteuses...

On eût dit la naissance d'un autre monde, n'étaient
le chatoiement des angoisses matricielles
et l'aboiement intolérable des cerbères
enchaînés aux pitons de l'Empire des Morts...

Mais rien, rien ne t'éprouve sur le chemin ascendant
tant ta tête s'élance en trait de jaspe purpurin
vers l'orée du Miracle...

Hind !

IN MEMORIAM

Hind!
Here, from the other end of night, the desert
mows
the shrapnel of its indigenous stars, whose every
beat exudes a myriad of errant lives...

Here, you will find no Hades, nor any Kokytos,
just an irisation of waters
inflamed into gentiana through your eyes,
a mirror from which the sky draws its tawny swan bath...

Gods with flaming blazons watch you, as you emerge from the depths
of eternal cataclysms,
clutching, between your fingers, the true symbols of Earth,
and the indomitable script that watermarks your soul...

As you loom closer, they form a single, sovereign guard...,
and above their helmeted heads
whirl the wings of age-old demons...

In a single breath they let loose
doves, their feathery down as exquisitely white and milky as opals...

It could have been the birth of another world, were it not
for the lustrous, anxious glow of the matrixes,
followed by the intolerable barking of Cerberus,
chained to the peaks of the Empire of the Dead...

But nothing, nothing tests you along your proceeding path
so much as your own head, soaring into a stroke of purple jasper,
on the cusp of a Miracle...

Hind!

C'est à l'heure où la planète se convulse
et se contorsionne dans la folie des hommes
que tu choisis le Retour...

Il n'est pire indigence que la honte millénaire
de ces êtres sans attache !

N'y-a-t-il pas le Liban, n'y-a-t-il pas la Palestine
éventrés par des sicaires ?

N'y-a-t-il pas l'Afrique de la faim et du sommeil ?

Hind !
Il y aura pourtant le printemps bleu de tes pas agiles
d'oryx
sillonnant les fondrières...

Il y aura le galet poli des mers du Sud
pareil à ton sourire ;
il y aura la musique que distille ton regard
à la lecture des quasars...
et la houlette de l'arganier rampant dans la rocaille...
et l'énorme troupeau de la houle sur les dents du déluge...

il y aura ici pour toi, pas un cénotaphe, mais une
mémoire
et toutes ces fleurs et même
le désert qui dans ta nuit hurle à la lune :
chevauchée ardente des fées vertes du Rêve,
ceignant pirogue pharaonique à Râ,

à l'heure où tout nivelle
les corps à l'armature du Temps
où tu te tiens debout sur un lit de roseaux.

Now is the hour when the planet contorts
and convulses in the madness of man,
whose Redemption is in your hands...

There's no greater indigence than the thousand-year-old shame
of these free-floating beings!

Does there remain a Lebanon, a Palestine
that the Sicarii have yet to disembowel?

Does there remain an Africa that isn't filled with famine and dreams?

Hind!
What there is is the blue spring of your every step, agile
as an oryx,
roaming the bogs...

What there is is the polished stone of the Southern seas,
reminiscent of your smile;
What there is is a music that will distribute your gaze
to the reader of quasars...
and the crook of the argan tree writhing through the scree...
and the enormous fold of the waves rolling along the deluge's teeth...

On its way for you is, not quite a cenotaph, but a
memory
of sorts, and all these flowers, and even
that desert, deep in your night, howling at the moon:
the fiery chevauchée of the Dream's verdant fairies,
girding Ra's pharaonic pirogue,

Now is the hour where everything reduces
bodies to the armature of Time;
where, over your bed of reeds, is you, and where you preside.

en cauris cinglés de seins, de hanches,
ceinte de la peau lisse des ténèbres ;
le baobab debout dans les calamités,
témoin des drames anciens ;
la piste de marbre et le dos roui d'étoiles
délétères
fouettant sur la rocaille l'esclave amer.

Wrought from cowry shells, clinging to hips, breasts, and thighs,

girdled by the shadows' smooth skin;

the baobab looming over the cataclysms,

witness to ancient dramas;

the marbled pathway and retted spine of the stars

slipped loose,

whipping the bitter slave into the gravel.

JOB

Certains marchent, euphoriques, sans savoir que la misère humaine, la misère ambiante s'accumule autour d'eux...Ils tentent de tout oublier...Ils prient, nez en l'air ou dans la gadoue...Lorsqu'ils longent des tombes, ils pleurent et frémissent pour se sauver dare-dare dans quelque drogue mentale que leurs endorphines et leurs phényléthylamines trament en neuroprocesseurs...

Leur cerveau n'est rien moins qu'un paquet de gélatine bleue. Et leur cœur une pompe qui irrigue un cadavre ambulant.

Voici :

Jérémie et les autres

Il y a la ville qui frémit, Apostropheur
retenu dans mon éclipse
lorsque je scalpe avec mon couteau d'obsidienne !

Prophète !
en vain j'essaye de te saisir
sur le crochet du scorpion,
tu m'échappes, tu es
vague et trop clair !

Planté en astre, incompris des staphylins,
les oiseaux t'abandonnent au rire
des filles
et te couvrent de leurs caresses insidieuses !

C'est l'examen frondeur
où je bâtis le Pleur et brise les Lois amères !

Qu'ils se souviennent de mes rides

JOB

Some go about their day in a state of euphoria, without noticing that human misery, that a clearly ambient misery, is accruing around them wherever they go…They try their best to forget everything…They utter prayers, their noses up in the air, or else down in the mire…While walking the tombs, they weep and shudder at the slightest provocation, seeking refuge in some mental intoxication that their endorphins and phenylethylamines go on weaving away at inside their neural processors…

A packet of blue gelatin, their brains; nothing more. Their heart, just a pump to irrigate a walking corpse.

Observe:

Jeremiah and the others

There it is, the quivering city, The Apostrophizer,
overtaken by my eclipse
as I head out, obsidian blade in hand, to collect my scalps!

Prophet!
In vain, I try seizing
the scorpion's hook;
you elude me, being
too obscure, too clear!

Driven to starlight, incomprehensible to the staphylinidae,
the birds abandon you to the amusement
of little girls
and smother you in their insidious caresses!

Such is the test, the insubordinate test
where I compile the Weeping and break the Bitter Laws!

May their memory cling to my wrinkled flesh,

Désarmeur de mes nerfs, qu'ils fourmillent en fucus !
Il y eut là, bleue, mon Etrenne,
le recueillement des fosses
et la Goule montée de la Rapière :

le tambour de Babylone,
Cercle précaire
où se réfracte la tectonique
hissant dans l'actinie le cheval janissaire...

Ils précédèrent l'ombre dessinée avec ma Larme,
debout sur le Galet,
j'étais la Forêt Morte escrimant sans merci
dans les catalepsies,
Soldat, vieux Soldat, lecteur gommant
le Vent, tu vas
sans retenue !

Prends-les comme Bételgeuse !
Il y a des nasses qui crient,
fongosités gisant dans les gibbosités !
Puisque je suis assis dans le Tonnerre,
puisque je suis debout sur un Galet
ainsi que le rayon insaisi du Soleil !

L'un me sangle les chiens,
la Bête immonde qui soutient
l'aura et la tornade...

L'autre brise la ville sans frimas ; Apostropheur,
retiens
le silence et la science
de l'Etre Amer !

Il n'y eut point de jérémiade, la Mer
éclata en synapses, en endorphines nuageuses

O nerve-disarmer, may they writhe in fucus!
There it was, in blue, my Strenna,
the recollection of gravesites,
and the Ghoul, mounted upon the Rapier:

The drum of Babylon,
the precarious Circle
where tectonics refract,
hoisting the janissary steed from the actinia...

They preceded the shadow, outlined in my Tear,
looming over the Pebble,
I was the Dead Forest fencing mercilessly
in catalepsy,
Soldier, old Soldier, O reader exfoliating
the Wind, how you proceed
without self-control!

Loom yourself into their beyond, like Betelgeuse!
Somewhere, the nassula is crying out;
the fungi, recumbently protruding!
For I am couched in Thunder,
for I loom over a Pebble,
elusively, like a ray of Sunlight!

One of them leashes the dogs,
the vile Beast upholding
both aura and tornado...

While the other tears through the frostless city; Apostrophizer,
withhold
the silence and the science
of Being's Bitterness!

There was no jeremiad to be had, the Sea
had already erupted into an array of synapses, into a cloud of endorphins,

et la houle drossée sur le rocher sédimentaire
peignit mon iris avec le bleu du Ciel...

Homme, je t'abandonne une peau mal écrite
où l'oléandre répète
la guerre réfractaire...
l'abîme maternel de l'Amidon
du Sang cruel !

Je te soumets la grille imprécise de Vénus,
cortège folâtre et beau
des excisions rompues sur la plante et sur l'or !

Souviens-toi de l'Etre Amer !

and the waves, propelled across the sedimentary soil,
painted my iris with the blueness of Sky…

Mankind, I leave an ill-scripted flesh in my wake,
a flesh where the oleander relives
its refractory warfare…,
the maternal abyss of Blood's
cruel Starch!

I offer you this, the imprecise grid of Venus,
the beautifully playful cortege
of excisions broken apart over the plants and the gold!

Never forget that Being is Bitterness!

L'ÉTRANGETÉ DU PASSANT

Arrimé à mon sang, je vois flamber la peau
des tonnerres qui s'étrillent en gerbes amères...
Le sable rira sur les vitraux de ma mémoire,
mais comme est dur l'hiver
planté en trident au mitan des étoiles !

Cercles, masques et frasques :
mimiques de pierres foulées par les miroirs,
vous êtes l'éclat du sol et n'était la roue faussée,
vous ne seriez qu'un brisant âpre,
une larme d'enfant assassiné.

Que le silence apprenne à vos paroles
ce temps où vous viviez d'insectes !
Un dieu vous signifia
les saisons mâles de la peur...

Arrimée à ma peau, elle inventa les luttes
— guerriers aux longues piques !
Ils carapacèrent de tortues les reîtres ternes...
Toute la piétaille croulait en rouissures...

La peur avait des lambeaux d'hommes dans les seins ;
les chevaux déferrés réimprimaient aux ascidies
les roches des abysses.
L'hysope et moi-même, ô rhizome, suivions
les spores du gyromitre.

Ils habitèrent ma peau bleue,
devinrent des stalagmites suppurantes ;
l'anthropoïde bardé de fer
cliqueta dans mes yeux.

THE STRANGENESS OF THE PASSERBY

Moored to my blood, I watch the fleshy thunderbolts
go up in flames, grooming themselves into bitter bouquets…
The sand will laugh against the stained-glass of my memory,
but how foreboding the winter is,
forking like a trident through the stars' midst!

Circles, masquerades, escapades:
mimicry of stones trampled by mirroring droves,
you who are the glow of the soil, and if not for the wheel's distortion
would live your life as nothing but one relentless breaker,
the teardrop of an assassinated child.

May the silence guide your speech back
to an age where you lived off insects!
To you, God meant
seasons of brutality, flourishing with fear…

Moored to my flesh, it dreamed up the struggle
—warriors with long lances!
They assumed tortoise formation, those lackluster reiters …
The entire rank and file crumbled into a flakey redness…

Fear had the last few remains of man inside its breast;
the unshod horses again pressed the abyssal boulders
down upon the ascidians.
The hyssop and I, O rhizome, followed
the spores of gyromitra.

They burrowed deep down into my blue skin,
transformed into festering stalagmites;
the iron-clad anthropoid
clanking away in my eyes.

La larme d'un enfant calcina les béryls ;
le lichen, le sourire crucial des chrysalides
se fit oiseau, très bel oiseau de mort.

Ouvrez donc mon cénotaphe !
Je suis la morsure du trigonocéphale,
le vent glacé du Pôle Céleste.
Vadrouillez dans ma peau froufroutant de roussettes ;
je suis ce fleuve suspendu
aux galaxies lointaines,
le neveu de Charon :
nautonier dont la rame brise le cuir du lac
quand les sorciers affichent le masque
éclairant des ténèbres.

Il n'est là qu'un roulement de tambours,
aucune issue, pas d'hypogée ;
le népenthès y croît librement dans la grisaille
comprimée par l'Ecrit savamment ordonné
de toutes les voix tues.

Les morts processionnaires y rampent,
à demi-nus parmi des crocs grinçants ;
ils laperont le sang
des Innocents.

Les vieilles amours croupissent
dans l'urne des ascidies ;
les grands socles bruissent
des sistoles d'un cœur maudit
et qui se blesse à l'or brûlé
des crépuscules opératoires.

Réinventé par l'ellipse des glèbes originales
et chromatiques,

The tear of the child burnt the beryl to ashes;
the lichen, the crucial smile of every chrysalis,
became a bird, the most exquisite bird of death.

Throw open this cenotaph of mine!
I am the trigonocephalus' teeth-marks,
the icy wind of the Celestial Pole.
Run your eyes over my flesh, swishing like hartouka;
I am this river suspended
from faraway galaxies,
Charon's nephew:
the helmsman whose oar breaks the leathery lake
as sorcerers hold up the mask
that shines through the shadows.

It's little more than a drum roll,
no escape, no hypogeum;
there, nepenthes grow freely in the gloom,
compressed by the Script, meticulously prepared
by a bevy of long-extinguished voices.

It's there that the dead processionaries writhe,
half-naked between squealing fangs;
on they go, lapping the blood
of the Innocents.

The old loves left to languish
in the ascidian urn;
the great plinths swell with the sound
of a damned heart's systoles,
and those stricken by the scorched gold
of crepuscular surgical theaters.

Reinvented by the ellipsis of the original and chromatic
glebes,

je parcours cet enfer
où ni le chant ancien qui brilla dans mes os
ni l'algue bleue fixée aux gènes considérables
des vies errantes,
aux photons, aux phéromones,
à la racine glanée au tréfonds des quasars,
aux quarks qui rayonnent
et pétillent dans mes rétines,
n'infirment le grimoire cunéiforme
des poussières d'où s'élève un cadavre inouï :
squelette de la Tribu vaste des Arachnides,
faucilles affilées sur les meules et les Tables
tournantes du Néant.

On infesta le Soleil de sarcoptes, de tétanies,
les chiens haineux de la nuit
écumèrent le pont et les cales des brigantins ;
ils avaient embouti le lemes, mon terroir
éclaté comme la chitine
des mantes abominables :

grouillement d'hoplites, de mercenaires et d'ilotes
que la Ténèbre crucifie ;
éléphants écrivant les peaux saignées
à blanc ;
javelots filant dans l'azur clair :
incendies de villes sempiternelles,
tueries si formidables que la Lune
n'éclaira de longtemps la rampe et que fuguèrent
les dieux impénitents du bocage mental ;

ainsi fut cette pierre préliminaire ;
la larme de la femme et de l'enfant,
les lionnes elles-mêmes rugirent
dès le commencement

I make the rounds of this hell,
where neither the ancient song that once glistened in my bones,
nor the blue seaweed holding on to the outstanding genes
of errant lives,
to the photons, the pheromones,
the root gleaned from the depths of quasars,
the quarks that radiate from
and sparkle from the insides of my eyes,
are enough to reject the cuneiform grimoire
of dust from which an unspeakable corpse arises:
the skeleton of the vast Tribe of Arachnids,
their sickles sharpened upon grindstones and rotary
Tables of Nothingness.

The Sun grew infested with scabies, with tetany,
and the wrath-filled hounds of night
cleaned out the deck and the holds of brigantines;
they had stamped out the lema, my locale
having exploded like the chitin
of abominable mantises:

a swarm of hoplites, of mercenaries and helots
crucified by Darkness;
elephants scribbling over bloody, obliterated
skins;
javelins spinning through the bright azure:
blazes of sempiternal cities,
slaughters so formidable that the Moon,
for a duration of time, refused to shine its guiding light and fled
the unrepentant gods of mental groves;

and so it was, this draft of stone;
the teardrop of woman and child,
the lionesses themselves, roaring
out, as soon as your memory-

des feux qui rongent ta mémoire.
Ils gravèrent au fronton du silicium la verte
et splendide chanson des Nombres inconnus ;
les clartés mutantes, les béquilles
et le legs fumant des constellations...

eating fires were lit.

They engraved the silicon pediment with the green

and splendid song of unknown Numbers;

its mutating clarities, its crutches,

and its legacy sending the constellations up in smoke…

REQUIEM

Trop de choses arrivèrent en même temps ;
l'inaccomplissement, la luxure — même la forme des choses
avait changé.
Ceux qui se voyaient dans un miroir avaient les yeux gelés.
Insectes fascinés, péremptoires :
ne sachant rien ni à qui offrir le Ciel, ils coururent
avec un rythme précaire...
ils coururent
sur nos dos...
Sommes-nous encore des dromadaires ?

Je suis ce Chien préliminaire,
ce laminaire et ce tonnerre, hormis
la foudre sillonnant fascinatrice l'éclair contus,
luxure si calme que mon sang torride et pur intente
aux sciences des léthargies
le pleur très noir du Lapidaire !

En ordonnée monté du Sable grain à grain,
depuis la Mer inamovible,
sorti de Moi Seul me fascinant Moi-Même !
en ces temps sinon morts du moins honnis
par ta Mémoire cruelle, Zénon !
Calculateur !

REQUIEM

Too many things were filling my head all at once;
a feeling of unfulfillment, lechery—the very shape of things themselves
had transformed.
Those who were looking in the mirror grew cold in the eyes.
Beguiled, peremptory insects:
not knowing to whom the Heavens were owed, they scurried away
in an uneasy rhythm...
they ran
up our backsides...
After all this time, are we still camels?

This lowly dog is what I am,
this laminaria, this thunderous boom, abreast of
the comely lightning crisscrossing the glow's contusion,
a lechery so tranquil that my blisteringly pure blood casts
the profoundly black tears of the Lapidary
at the feet of lethargy's science!

Along the ordinate and up the Sand, grain by grain,
beyond the unmovable sea,
My own Self-dazzling Self escapes,
through this dead and lowly age,
the cruelty of your Memory, O Zeno,
O Calculator!

SAIGNÉE D'ÉTOILES

Iconoclaste tribu, engeance ignominieuse !
Quand tout s'agite, quand tout s'excite,
la parole à l'envers du nopal tient les griffes
des pupilles et des lames...

Asparagus saignant jonchée d'astres, tu vois
le soleil cuit à point :
surgeon retourné sur le puits mauvais et fort...
Tu vois la Terre radieuse,

ces planètes
écrasées dans l'œil précaire
du céraste, locataire du verre dicté
à l'exclusion des cœurs roidis...

dicté au sommeil étincelant, aux cailloux nègres.
Il est une larme, ô tourterelle,
sur le fil des mers suantes !
Elle mesure

l'encoignure des tes naissances.

THE BLOODLETTING OF THE STARS

Iconoclastic tribe, ignominious brood!
While chaos rears its head, while everything's on-edge,
the word inside the nopal conducts the claws
of pupils and blades...

O bloody asparagus strewn with stars, you watch
the well-seared sun:
sprouts rounding the well, wicked and strong...
You watch the Earth's radiance,

those planets,
crushed into the viper's
precarious eye, a glassy residence dictated
over a heartless absence...,

over dreams, over glistening dreams, over the darkening scree.
It takes the shape of a teardrop, O turtledove,
down the finer edge of the dulled seas!
doling out

the angle of your emergences.

CHAMELIER FOU

Chamelier, ta caravane sera la lame
et l'écume
du pisé huant l'hélium :
une orchidée noire de quasars ;

le jeu du colibri
et la lunette de Galilée :
Galilei Galileo, voici fleurir l'inquisition
sorcière !

Les calendes détonent en le cri fétide des morts;
c'est l'insolence des crapauds,
la vitre et la nuit mal cousue des oiseaux...

C'est à claquer du bec
parmi tes miroirs fauves,
si pathétique Gorée,
debout
sur l'enfance du soleil,
chemineau des épactes,
comme toi, vieux chamelier allant, venant
parmi les tourterelles
et le calendrier magnifique de la Terre.

Je les couvris de pustules,
crapauds amarrés à mon sang ordinaire,
aux phalènes, aux éphémères ;

c'est la Glose d'un autre Ciel
courbé par les ailes d'un vieil élémentaire.

DISORIENTED CAMEL-DRIVER

Camel-driver, may your caravan be the sword
and scum
of the bellowing helium of adobe:
a black orchid of quasars,

the plaything of the hummingbird,
and the optics of Galileo:
O Galileo Galilei, behold the bloom of the witching
inquisition!

The calends detonates into the noxious screams of dead men;
It is the insolence of toads,
windows, and night's crudely-woven birds...

It is the clattering of beaks
scattered throughout your tawny mirrors,
Gorée, pitifully
looming
over the sun's youth,
driving the vagrancy of epactae,
like you, timeless camel-driver, appearing and disappearing,
rounding the turtledoves
and the magnificent calendar of the Earth.

Every toad moored to this blood of mine,
to the moths, and to the mayflies, I've drowned
in warts;

it is the Gloss of some other Sky,
warped by the wings of an age-old elemental.

RÉCURRENCES
à Lahbib M'seffer

Couvées phosphorescentes des colombes,
il est un temps d'étoiles récurrentes :
réquisitoire gagé...

il pagaie dans ta jouvence,
simulie qui de mon or ramène
les cartons du silence...

Cette houle n'était pas claire ; les temps comptés
laminaient le ciel fin ;

"Habille-toi de bure ! Mal ordinaire."

La mer elle-même écoute
l'arc bandé des novae.

RECOURSES

for Lahbib M'Seffer

O brood of doves, versed in phosphorescence,
now is the time of the stars' recourse;
the requisition, once pledged…

see how they row through your youth: those oars,
that simulium circling back from my gold,
silence in tow…

Its swell, just a blur; the dwelling atmosphere
would roll the sky out, in sheets;

"Drape yourself in this habit!, O habitual evil."

The sea itself awaits the sound
of a nova's drawn bow.

ABOUT THE AUTHOR

Mohammed Khaïr-Eddine was born in 1941 near Tafraout, Southern Morocco, of Amazigh heritage. One of the original co-founders of the revolutionary Maghrebi review *Souffles-Anfas*, alongside Abdellatif Laâbi and Mostafa Nissaboury, he is today renowned for what he coined his "linguistic guerrilla warfare": an incendiary, surrealist-inspired, and iconoclastic writing style. The author of numerous volumes of prose, poetry, and drama, his full-length works include *Agadir* (1967); *Corps négatif, suivi de Histoire d'un Bon Dieu* (1968); *Soleil arachnide* (1969); *Moi, L'aigre* (1970); *Le Déterreur* (1973); *Ce Maroc !* (1975), *Une odeur de mantèque* (1976), and *Résurrection des fleurs sauvages* (1981, 1994), among others. He lived in self-exile in France beginning in 1965, returning to Morocco only in 1979. Khaïr-Eddine died in Rabat on November 18, 1995— Independence Day in Morocco.

ABOUT THE TRANSLATOR

Jake Syersak is a poet, translator, and editor. He holds an MFA in Creative Writing from the University of Arizona and a PhD in English and Creative Writing from the University of Georgia. He is author of the poetry collections *Mantic Compost* (Trembling Pillow Press, 2022) and *Yield Architecture* (Burnside Review Books, 2018). He is the co-translator, with Pierre Joris, of Mohammed Khaïr-Eddine's hybrid novel *Agadir* (Diálogos Press, 2020). Forthcoming translations include the Mohammed Khaïr-Eddine's *I, Caustic* (Litmus Press, 2022) and *Proximal Morocco—* (Ugly Duckling Presse, 2023).

ABOUT THE PRESS

OOMPH! is an international literary press publishing contemporary poetry and short prose in translation. Editors Daniel Beauregard and Alex Gregor founded the press in 2014 with one aim in mind—to find new literature written in countries around the world and facilitate its translation into English. The editorial team currently operates in Buenos Aires, Argentina and Rome, Italy to realize this goal as part of a larger mission to encourage cross-cultural and -linguistic exchange. Find out more at www.oomphpress.com

Contemporary Works Vol. III:
A Multilingual Anthology

Jahan Khajavi

Mike Corrao

Germán Sierra

Vi Khi Nao

Jessica Sequeira

Laura Cozma (trans. from the Romanian by Cristina Savin)

James Knight

Cristián Gómez Olivares (trans. from the Spanish by Ilana Luna)

Kim Vodicka

Mohammed Khaïr-Eddine (trans. from the French by Jake Syersak)

Brandon Shimoda

Ava Hofmann

Gaspar Orozco (trans. from the Spanish by Ilana Luna)

David Kuhnlein

Shahin Sadeghzadeh (trans. from the Farsi by Khashayar Mohammadi)

Klara du Plessis

Shane Jesse Christmass

Carlos Soto Román

Tilde Acuña (trans. from the Filipino by Kristine Ong Muslim)

Evan Isoline

Daniel Scott Tysdal

Marston Hefner

Julia Otxoa (trans. from the Spanish by A. Stickley, B. Newhard, and M. Truckenmiller Saylor)

Victoria Mbabazi

Souad Labbize (trans. from the French by Susanna Lang)

Matt Lee

Vasile Baghiu (trans. from the Romanian by Cristina Savin)

Paul Bisagni

r.g. vasicek

yours truly, the happy recluse

Charlene Elsby and Lindsay Lerman

Dimitry Galkovsky (trans. from the Russian by Alexander Sharov)

Contemporary Works In Translation:
A Multilingual Anthology (Vol. I)

Laura Vazquez (trans. by Evan Leed)
Daniel Blanchard (trans. by JD Larson)
Friederike Mayröcker (trans. by JD Larson)
Yorlady Ruíz López (trans. by Emily Paskevics)
Sara Tuss Efrik (trans. by Paul Cunningham)
Sofia Roberg (trans. by Nicholas Lawrence)
Rodrigo Lira (trans. by Thomas Rothe & Rodrigo Olavarría)
Véronique Pittolo (trans. by Laura Mullen)
Nasser Rabah (trans. by Joanna Chen & Julie Yelle)
Yonatan Berg (trans. by Joanna Chen)
Laura Wittner (trans. by Shira Rubenstein)
Roberta Iannamico (trans. by Alexis Almeida)
Roberto Barbery (trans. by Evan Leed)
Olja Savičević Ivančević (trans. by Andrea Jurjevic)

Contemporary Works In Translation:
A Multilingual Anthology (Vol. II)

Jaime Pinos (trans. by Carlos Soto Román)
Giorgia Romagnoli (trans. by Giorgia Romagnoli)
Mohammed Khaïr-Eddine (trans. by Jake Syersak)
Marco Giovenale (trans. by Diana Thow)
Alessandro De Francesco (trans. by Andreas Burckhardt)
Nurit Kasztelan (trans. by Francesca Cricelli)
Florinda Fusco (trans. by Jean-luc Defromont)
Martín Armada (trans. by Shira Rubenstein)
Diego Alfaro Palma (trans. by Lucian Mattison)
Liliana Moreno Muñoz (trans. by Emily Paskevics)
Alessandra Greco (trans. by Marcella Greco)
Claudio Bertoni (trans. by Carlos Soto Román)
Maria Grazia Calandrone (trans. by Johanna Bishop)
Marina Yuszczuk (trans. by Alexis Almeida)
Giancarlo Huapaya (trans. by Ilana Luna)
Andrea Inglese (trans. by Sara Elena Rossetti)

Melismas

Written by Marlon Hacla
Translated from the Filipino by Kristine Ong Muslim
Illustrated by Tilde Acuña
Introduction by Amado Anthony G. Mendoza III

"What's most distinguished in Marlon Hacla's *Melismas* is sincere invocation—'This is how I will carry on: lightning storm that enters a creek, dyed seraphim, bottled scorpion,' its indisputable inaugurations of pressure and freedom—'split the violins with an ax,' breaching form into form the riddled rhythms of our ageless Age of Noise, proletarian and industrial, domesticated and ferocious, are all 'upright pickets' 'worshipped by sound.'"

—Marchiesal Bustamante, author of *Mulligan* (High Chair)

Words

Written by Helena Österlund
Translated from Swedish by Paul Cunningham

"Cunningham's translations from Helena Österlund's *Words and Colors* bring us crystal stinging incantations amidst the teeth and foliage that permeate consciousness. He conveys the precision and full-bloodedness of Österlund's mesmeric demarcations between belief, certainty, and uncertainty, and these poems make readers pitch desperately towards their own ideas about bodily senses and the language that marks desire, will, and the natural world that exists and acts. I am marked by these poems, I am shattered and sprung from these poems, and I am so grateful to Cunningham for providing me entrance to these poems."

—Ginger Ko, author of *Inherit* (Sidebrow)

First Breaths

Written by Mohammed Khaïr-Eddine
Translated from the French by Jake Syersak

"'I didn't vomit / the pistol-like word which is fearless.'" I'm grateful to Jake Syersak for continuing to bring Moroccan poet Mohammed Khaïr-Eddine's work into English. These poems are written with the greatest intensity and urgency. They are angry and political, but they are also deliriously intoxicated with language and its possibilities."

—Johannes Göransson author of *Transgressive Circulation:*
Essays On Translation (Noemi Press)